# JUST ASK

## VOLUME THREE

## DOUG NEWTON

Mary's Place Publishing
Greenville, Illinois

Just Ask: Volume Three
© 2016 by Douglas Newton

Published by Mary's Place Publishing
a division of Mary's Place, Inc.
Mailing Address:
1302 Lake Shore Dr.
Greenville, IL 62246

Printed in the United States of America

ISBN 978-0-9973380-0-3

For information about all releases from Mary's Place Publishing visit our website at www.marysplace.org.

To my Dad and Mom who required me by wisdom and
to my Lord who inspired me by example
to do what may be the hardest thing for any writer:
finish what I started.

# CONTENTS

# PREFACE

The original idea for the three volume *Just Ask* series came to me in the shower one morning. For some reason lots of people experience moments of inspiration in the shower. One day the Lord may explain to us why that is the case. Nevertheless that's where it happened, and I instantly knew I had to take on this project.

However, that was the moment of inspiration for writing the series only. The moment of inspiration for the perspective behind this series and particularly the use of the word "just" in *Just Ask* came more than 20 years before that. Here's when it happened...

I was preparing a lesson on prayer using the famous portion of scripture where the disciples asked Jesus, "Teach us to pray" (Luke 11:1). As I imagined that situation, and what Jesus said in response, I pictured the disciples picking up pens and paper to take notes on what they expected would be a verbal stream of complicated theological insights. After all libraries of books have been written about it! Instead, I imagined Jesus saying, "Put your pens down. You don't need to take notes. Just listen. If you really get what I'm about to tell you, you'll never forget it."

Then He proceeded to make three simple points. He gave them a brief pattern for prayer that we now call the "Lord's Prayer." He shared a short parable about going to a friend at midnight with a request for help for another friend in desperate need. Then He topped off His lesson on prayer with a famous conclusion emphasizing three verbs: ask, seek, knock. For English language speakers the first letter of each word conveniently spells A.S.K. Could it be any simpler?

Jesus underscored His lesson with a brief explanation for its simplicity: It's all because of how much your heavenly Father loves you.

That was a turning point moment in my life. And Jesus was right. I didn't need to take any notes. I got it. And I can never forget it. When my theological mind wants to complicate the matter of prayer, Jesus bends me back toward the basic rule: Just ask.

To be sure, from that point of simplicity it is worthwhile plumbing the depths of prayer, asking questions about the proper balance between petition and praise. There's nothing wrong with exploring the role of faith or divine sovereignty in relation to prayer. It's helpful listening to others explain their approach to the discipline of prayer, or their caution about not treating God like a vending machine, as my author friend Marv Hinten once wrote about.

There are many things to be taught and learned in response to the question, "Teach us how to pray." But it is too often overlooked that the disciples did not ask that question. They asked, "Teach us to pray." They weren't asking the how question.

Jesus' answer reveals what He must have considered the chief impediment to a life of prayer: the failure to understand how good and ready God is to meet us and our needs if we just ask.

That word "just" creates a grace explosion in my mind. It tells me everything I need to know about God's love and how to approach prayer. In his classic book *Prayer*, Ole Hallesby points out that true prayer arises fundamentally from a spirit of helplessness. When we are at a complete loss, there is only one thing that is necessary to find help in our time of need: just ask.

Ironically, this book completes the three volumes totalling more than 400 pages and 180,000 words, but their take away message boils down to the two biggest and boldest words on each cover: JUST ASK. If my readers would take the Lord at His word and do that, my mission would be fulfilled.

In light of that I would like to extend one more huge thank you to my congregation, staff and leaders at the Greenville (IL) Free Methodist Church. The three month sabbatical they gave me, that I chose to spread out one month at a time over three years, was a great privilege. Many of our folks are walking with my wife and me toward becoming a true house of prayer. It is a tremedous gift to have their support through encouragement and prayer. I have tried to honor their gift through the faithful completion of the original vision.

Finally, I will never be able to express enough thanks to my family and especially my wife Margie—my prayer partner and model—for their constant support.

*JANUARY 2016*

# INTRODUCTION

PICTURE A PERSON TAKING a high-powered telescope outside on a clear night to get a close up look at Saturn. That's not an easy thing to do. It takes a lot of setup and careful calibration to dial in the telescope's orientation and focus. Once you do that you get to see something that takes your breath away.

That's what this book is like. I want to show you some things about salvation that will take your breath away. But first I must spend three preliminary chapters recalibrating your orientation...

Now that you know where I'm going, let me make sure you know where I am coming from. In all three *Just Ask* volumes I am answering the question "How can a person be more confident in prayer?" This is an important question because confidence (or bold faith) seems to be a requirement for fervent and effective prayer.

The old King James still echoes across the ages: "The effectual fervent prayer of a righteous man availeth much" (James 5:16). It guarantees us that God will give any seeker divine wisdom under one condition: "But let him ask in faith, nothing wavering" (James 1:6). No matter what our situation we are invited to "come boldly unto the throne of grace, that we may obtain mercy, and find grace to help in time of need" (Hebrews 4:16).

I could cite numerous other references to the importance of confidence, faith, boldness and perseverance. The sheer number of these exhortations leaves our ears ringing with the message: Pray confidently.

Then when we add to the mix Jesus' numerous invitations to "ask whatever" (a phrase we examined in *Volume One*) suddenly we have an additional reason to doubt whether we are praying proper prayers. The challenge to pray boldly along with Jesus' incredibly wide-open invitation leaves us second-guessing ourselves.

My mission is to relieve those worries and uncertainties by playing a role in the reader's life that is similar to what my wife's college roommate played in

bringing us together in marriage. My normal uncertainty and hesitation to ask Margie out on our first date was insurmountable until her roommate assured me, "I've talked to Margie and I'm sure she will say *yes* if you ask." Her input gave me the boldness to ask and our current 41 years of marriage is the direct result.

The strategic method of this book is exactly the same: I'll be like my wife's roommate for the reader. I am giving you insight into what God is interested in doing, so that you will have greater confidence God will say *yes* to your prayers. How am I providing these insights? By offering a more comprehensive view of salvation than we typically see.

God's plan of salvation offers the clearest picture of what's in God's heart. The problem is that most Christians have been taught to view salvation from a narrow point of view: the *judicial paradigm*, which summarizes salvation as Christ paying for our sins so we can be forgiven and live forever. Of course that is true, but it is only one way—or *paradigm* as we have been calling it—to look at salvation.

The Bible offers many other ways to look at salvation and what God was accomplishing through the death and resurrection of Jesus Christ. In all three volumes I am arguing that by examining and understanding salvation through these different paradigms, we get a much fuller picture of the heart of God and consequently much greater clarity concerning how we can pray confidently.

So for example, not only does salvation provide payment for sins (judicial paradigm), it also is helping people who are absolutely lost find meaning, identity and purpose (lost and found paradigm). Salvation is also about bringing people back into the presence of God (presence paradigm) and making them one with the Father (union paradigm). Salvation can also be seen from the angle of rescuing the world from the dominion of Satan (victory paradigm) and reversing the curse of hard, fruitless labor (abundance paradigm). The cross of Jesus Christ also restores people to their original source of righteous living (moral transformation paradigm) and fixes all the areas of brokenness that make them less than whole (healing paradigm.) Looking at salvation through these lenses broadens and enriches our awareness of what God wanted desperately enough to send His Son to die on the cross and, therefore, what He must continue to want even now.

In short, the *Just Ask* series teaches confident prayer through seeing the purposes of God reflected in the greatness of salvation. As I studied these various paradigms I noticed that they seemed to fit nicely into three categories: reconciliation (*Volume One*), redemption (*Volume Two*) and revelation (*Volume Three*).

If this recap of the purpose and trajectory of the *Just Ask* series is too brief or still leaves you with questions, you can try reading the introduction and first three chapters of *Volume One*. There is also an appendix section at the end of *Volume Two* that provides selected quotes from the early chapters of *Volume One*.

Finally, this series is not called *Just Think* as if new and stimulating thoughts is all we need. The purpose of *Just Ask* is to help you pray more confidently. That's why each of the chapters that examines a paradigm concludes with an application section including summaries, questions, related situations and sample prayers to help you practice what you've just read.

If you're a normal human being you'll be tempted to skim through those pages or even skip right over them. But I urge you to spend some time lingering in meditation with the help of the Holy Spirit. Those questions and samples will help you see just how the paradigm translates into appropriate prayers.

As of writing this volume, the previous two volumes have been out for a couple of years. Often I hear about the *Just Ask* books being used in churches and small groups. Perhaps that could help you engage more meaningfully in the application section. Get with two or three friends in a short-term group and go through the books together.

I can confidently predict that in the process you will practice praying more confidently and see more prayers answered as a result. That in turn builds your confidence even more to pray broadly and boldly, resulting in more answers. It will be like you're climbing a spiral staircase upward toward greater faith and love for God. All because you're learning to just ask.

# CHAPTER ONE

# Little Do We Know

KEN BARUN LAY BENEATH AN OVERPASS in Houston, Texas, strung out on heroine when a Catholic nun found him and got him into a treatment facility. Little did she know what would result from this one act of rescue nor what would become of this young man's life.

Ken grew up as a Jew in New York City. His orthodox parents disowned him and kicked him out of the house at sixteen due to his addiction. But before that time, Ken's dad, though orthodox, always insisted that his family gather around the TV whenever a Billy Graham crusade came on. Little did Billy Graham or Ken's parents know what would become of this young man's life.

After time in treatment at the drug rehab center, Ken grabbed hold of his life, followed the program, and succeeded in breaking his addiction. Eventually he came to direct the program there and also start a few businesses for the residents to learn skills and find opportunities for self-improvement.

That's when somehow Ronald and Nancy Reagan heard about the

Houston center (someone must have written a letter) and decided they should visit. Whoever wrote that letter to them… little did they know what would become of this young man's life.

The Reagan's were impressed by Ken and invited him to come work at the White House as Director of Projects and Policies. Didn't they know he was a recovering drug addict? Yes, they knew that. But little did they know how taking a chance on him would affect the world.

After his time at the White House working and traveling with the Reagan's inner circle, Ken Barun took a position with McDonald's corporation. Eventually, Ken was asked to develop charitable enterprises for the corporation and created the Ronald McDonald House with a $300,000 investment. It grew into a 1.8 billion dollar foundation. Then he was appointed to head the McDonald's nutrition division at a time the company was under fire from documentaries such as "Super-Size Me" over its alleged contribution to obesity in America. It was Ken who introduced healthier items such as fruits, salads and parfaits to McDonald's menu.

Ultimately Ken became Senior Executive Vice President. Amazing! Little did that Catholic nun or anyone else know... But all this time there was one other thing Ken Barun did not know: Jesus Christ as his Savior.

It goes without saying that Ken was running in business and social circles of the highest order. One day while driving a Ferrari around the country in a charity race, his car partner kept egging him on to drive faster and faster.

Ken hesitated, "Obviously you're not afraid to die."

"That's because I know where I'm going when I die; I have an eternal relationship with Jesus Christ," he said.

Ken didn't want to hear any more and slammed the brakes on the conversation quickly. However, his friend Paul never gave up on him.

Ten years later Ken and Paul were sitting at a restaurant when Ken opened up about his life being both full of good things yet lacking something he could not identify. Though he had never heard the phrase before, he spoke of a "hole in his heart."

> Didn't they know he was a recovering drug addict? Yes, they knew that. But little did they know how taking a chance on him would affect the world.

Paul saw the opening and invited Ken to pray right there in the restaurant to ask Jesus Christ to fill his life. Ken responded quickly. His tears flowed freely. The owner came over, worried the food had been horrible. Little did he, or Paul, or even Ken know what would come of that moment.

Ken grew in his faith and boldness. But some of his new-found practices, like opening staff meetings with prayer, did not fit the McDonald's corporate culture. So eventually Ken knew it was time to move on. Where? He did not know.

The very day Ken quit he got a call from Paul who mentioned he was on the board of Franklin Graham's "Samaritan's Purse" organization. "How about coming here and helping us?" Paul asked.

Initially Ken balked but soon changed his mind. One thing led to another and Ken eventually became chief of staff for the Billy Graham Evangelistic Association, charged with leading the organization through the challenges of transition into a future without the world famous evangelist as its prominent public face.

Isn't this all amazing! A Jewish dad insisted that his children, one of whom becomes a homeless drug addict, watch a Jesus-preaching television evangelist. Then one day forty years later that very son became a key leader in that very ministry. Little did anyone know!

> We all live lives that God is directing toward unpredictable goals.

There is a pattern to this story that is shared by all of us. While it may not result in such a dramatic turnaround, we all live lives that God is directing toward unpredictable goals. At any given point in time each of us could and should probably acknowledge "little do we know" where things will wind up.

That got me thinking about many of the most famous Bible stories. They all share this pattern as well. Little did people know as they were going through the events of their lives that there was more going on than met the eye. Perhaps the most astounding and wonderful example involved the people connected with the birth of Jesus.

THE UNPREDICTABLE JESUS

When you think about it, everyone involved in the birth of Jesus—the coming of the Son of God in the flesh—had no clear idea what was going on. Sure, Joseph had been tipped off by an angel...

> *An angel of the Lord appeared to Joseph in a dream and said, "Joseph son of David, do not be afraid to take Mary home as your wife, because what is conceived in her is from the Holy Spirit. She will give birth to a son, and you are to give him the name Jesus, because he will save his people from their sins."* Matthew 1:20-21

But little did he know... He couldn't even begin to imagine.

Mary had also been notified by angelic visitation, of course...

> *But the angel said to her, "Do not be afraid, Mary, you have found favor with God. You will be with child and give birth to a son, and you are to give him the name Jesus. He will be great and will be called the Son of the Most High. The Lord God will give him the throne of his father David, and he will reign over the house of Jacob forever; his kingdom will never end."*
>
> *"How will this be," Mary asked the angel, "since I am a virgin?"*
>
> *The angel answered, "The Holy Spirit will come upon you, and the power of the Most High will overshadow you. So the holy one to be born will be called the Son of God.* Luke 1:30-35

But little did she know all that was going on. One of the many popular Christmas songs points this out beautifully;

> *Mary did you know that your baby boy will one day walk on water?*
> *Mary did you know that your baby boy will save our sons and daughters?*
> *Did you know that your baby boy has come to make you new?*
> *This child that you've delivered, will soon deliver you.*

I'm sure she heard the message of the angels and she understood what their words meant, but how could she have really known…?

From her point of view, when she and Joseph arrived in Bethlehem, she could not have known how God's plan was for Jesus to identify with all the lowly people of the world. All she could see was the inn's no vacancy sign and that there was no place for her to give birth except in a stable. Things did not appear to be going well. But little did she know…

And how could the innkeeper who turned them away have known what he was doing? Little did he know this baby was the Messiah.

And what about the shepherds. I wonder what one of them might have reminisced some years after that night…

*I remember walking down this very path that night after hearing the angel's message about the birth of the Messiah. All I could think about was "I can't believe this is happening to me!"*

*But I never would have guessed that night what else would happen years later. There really wasn't any particular evidence of a Savior being born, like the angels said. I mean…you know… when I got to the manger…sure, here was this baby. But nothing else. Nothing more than you would expect. He was a baby. He had no clue I was there. He was sleeping the whole time. His mother was rocking him, kind of humming under her breath. All in all it wouldn't have been spectacular without the angels.*

*But I wish I had known then what I know now. Don't get me wrong. When I saw him I knelt down with the other guys, but I'm not sure my heart was in it. All I had to go on was what the angels said, but I really had no clue what they meant. But now?... I wish I could do it all over again. Because now I know. I mean, now I understand who this little baby was. My goodness, if I had known I wouldn't have just knelt down, kind of going through the motions, I would have really knelt down! I would have given my whole life to Him right there on the spot. But little did I know.*

The biblical record reveals that virtually everyone involved had some knowledge but not enough to really understand the full meaning of everything going on around them. Little did they know.

## LITTLE DID I KNOW

That got me thinking about my life and how I have wound up writing this book. While I was going through my post college years and then my early years in marriage and ministry, my life route seemed erratic. Almost everything I wound up doing appeared to follow a path of *coincidence*.

The event that led to my becoming a pastor occurred one day when I was applying to be a magazine editor and *just happened* to have an impromptu lunch with a former professor during a break from my interview. He made a *passing comment* about a unique philosophy graduate program, but quickly added, "I know you wouln't be interested in relocating to a university 700 miles away."

What seemed to be a circuitous route as I lived the journey turned out to be the way God draws a straight line to His purposes.

However, when he saw my "not so fast" facial expression—which he wouldn't have seen had I not been sitting across the table from him—he immediately made a phone call to the dean of the department. On the spot I was accepted into the program with a full scholarship and a position as a teaching assistant in English.

That unexpectedly led to my becoming a short-term student pastor at a small church that grew large enough to shift my attention to a calling I did not yet know I had. My "short-term" pastorate lasted thirteen years.

On occasions I would be asked to speak at special events around the region, which led to my being asked to speak a few times at a Christian boarding school three hours away, which led to my being asked to serve as its president—something I had no plans or formal training to do.

That role led to my being on the road off and on for five years promoting the school, but also speaking at colleges and camps. This led to my being "noticed" by our denominational bishops, who asked me to be the editor of our denominational magazine. Which led to… Which led to… Which led to… And now I am here.

What seemed to be a circuitous route as I lived the journey turned out to be the way God draws a straight line to His purposes. Little did I know.

## IT'S ALREADY HAPPENING!

When I put all of this together—the life of Ken Barun, the life of Mary and Joseph, the life of Doug Newton, and most likely yours as well—I find myself drawn to look at one verse in scripture from a new angle. It is a verse in scripture that you probably have read or heard many times. It's a praise benediction found in Ephesians that goes like this:

*Now to him who is able to do immeasurably more than all we ask or imagine, according to his power that is at work within us, to him be glory in the church and in Christ Jesus throughout all generations, for ever and ever! Amen.*  Ephesians 3:20-21

Isn't that wonderful! God is "able to do immeasurably more than all we ask or imagine." But if we really understand what was going on with the birth of Jesus Christ, how everyone involved had only limited understanding of what they were involved in, if we really understand that, then we must also say that God is *not only able to do* more than we ask or imagine, He is at any given moment *already doing* more than we ask or imagine.

Right now. In your life. Even if it looks like you're just being turned away at an innkeeper's door. God is already doing more than you ask or imagine. Right now. In your life. Even though you may feel like you're only out working in the fields of a daily grind, God is already doing more than you ask or imagine.

We, all of us, live in the middle of a "little do we know" story of God's plans. He is not only able to do immeasurably more than all we ask or imagine, He is already doing it.

However—and this is a big however—on some occasions God is very eager to give us a glimpse into what He has going on. He reveals where things are headed, at least in part. He forecasts.

For example, He took Abraham out into the cool night air, directed his gaze to the stars in the heavens above, and revealed what the future would hold for him:

> But Abram said, "O Sovereign Lord, what can you give me since I remain childless and the one who will inherit my estate is Eliezer of Damascus?" And Abram said, "You have given me no children; so a servant in my household will be my heir."
>
> Then the word of the Lord came to him: "This man will not be your heir, but a son coming from your own body will be your heir." He took him outside and said, "Look up at the heavens and count the stars—if indeed you can count them." Then he said to him, "So shall your offspring be."   Genesis 15:2-5

Then scripture concludes that story with the central doctrinal lesson of the Christian faith: Abram believed the Lord, and he credited it to him as righteousness. Saving faith involves not just believing God about the cross of Jesus Christ, but believing him about everything. Here it pertains particularly— and for the first time in history—to believing God's revelation about his future plans. Believing that at any given point in time God has something going on that goes beyond what we can ask or imagine!

And even though God is in charge of when He reveals those things, isn't this exactly what He invites us to seek Him for?

> This is what the Lord says, he who made the earth, the Lord who formed it and established it—the Lord is his name: "Call to me and I will answer you and **tell you great and unsearchable things you do not know.**"   Jeremiah 33:2-3

If it is the case that God invites us to seek Him for revelation about what He is up to, and if He is always up to something beyond what we currently know or imagine, might this not—should this not—also inform how we begin to look at His work of salvation on the cross?

When we think about salvation we often look backward rather than forward. We think of the cross as God's plan to correct problems. It's about restoring what was lost or broken, and rightly so. The cross corrects the problem of sin and evil run amok. It corrects the problem of human brokenness and hopelessness. But what if we look forward rather than backward? What if the cross was as much about new things God would create as about wrong things He would correct?

What if the purpose of the cross was to create new possibilities and make available things never before attainable?

> What if the cross was as much about new things God would create as about wrong things He would correct?

## GLORY REVEALED THROUGH CREATION

It is often suggested that the purpose of the cross was to restore humankind to God's original purpose in the Garden of Eden. Indeed, I made much of that idea in Volumes One and Two. But what if God, when His Son died on the cross, had in mind creating something He had not yet finished at the moment He created the garden and placed mankind in it? What if salvation is moving toward something brand new.

Doesn't this make sense after all? God is the Creator. He glorifies Himself through what He creates. It is His desire to reveal His glory through His wonderful works. Many of the psalms, like Psalm 19 for example,  make this clear:

> The **heavens declare the glory of God;**
> the skies proclaim the work of his hands.   Psalm 19:1

It doesn't make sense if God wants to display His glory around the universe through His works of creation that He would have stopped creating after the Sixth Day. Instead it makes so much more sense to think "once a creator always a creator" and believe that God, the Creator, is still creating. He is still doing "great and unsearchable things" to reveal His glory.

In this third volume of the *Just Ask* series, we will turn our eyes forward. We will spin around 180 degrees at the foot of the cross and see what salvation means by looking toward the future to see what God might have going on that brings about things that never existed before the cross.

For example, in chapter four and five we will see that He is bringing more glory to Himself by creating a brand new, never-before-imagined kind of human being. In chapter six we'll consider the brand new, never-before-imagined holy community He's creating, and top it off in chapter seven with a look at the brand new, never-before-imagined world we're heading for.

All through the Bible God gives us glimpses into what He wants to create—something new that He is wanting to do. God is not just restoring things to a former glory, but He is taking things to a new glory. He is doing more works of creation to *reveal* His glory. Some of those things—things His saving work made possible— will not happen until the end of time as we know it. That means His salvation is not complete until those things occur. But not all of those unfulfilled plans must wait on a particular date and time in the eschatological future. Some of them will occur now as we work in partnership with God.

In summary, this final *Just Ask* volume examines what can be grouped together under the title *revelation paradigms*—ways to look at salvation that help us see God's new glory-revealing works of creation that we have a role in. Even though we live in the midst of "little do we know" events, sometimes God shows us "great and unsearchable things" and we get to be involved. Especially through prayer. Not only will He do immeasurably more than we ask or imagine, He already is. Feast on this one last example.

## HISTORY OF "O HOLY NIGHT"

In 1847 the commissioner of wines in a small French town was asked to write a poem for Christmas by the local priest. It was a surprising request, because everyone knew Placide Cappeau de Roquemaure was not much of a church-goer. Why did the priest ask him? No one knows, not even Cappeau, and perhaps not even the priest.

However, he enjoyed poetry. And because he was enough of a romantic that the nativity story captured his imagination even if its babe had never fully captured his heart, the words of the poem flowed easily one day while traveling a bumpy road to Paris. The familiar words of Luke's gospel led his imagination like a star toward that night in Bethlehem, as if he were a witness at the blessed moment. And before his coach arrived in the City of Light, Cappeau had completed "Cantique de Noel"—the Song of Christmas.

He was struck by what he had written, as if it was more than a poem. Something about it demanded greater reverence; *It should be set to music.* So he contacted one of his friends, an accomplished and well-known composer, Adolphe Charles Adams. "Would you set this poem to music?" he asked.

Adams frequently received these kinds of requests from orchestras and ballets all over the world. But a poem? However, after reading it, he couldn't refuse, even though it exalted a day he did not celebrate and a savior he did not acknowledge. You see, Adams was Jewish.

Within three weeks the beautiful song was complete and had already been performed at the Midnight Mass on Christmas Eve. The public found it to be so moving that the song quickly filled the sanctuaries of many churches in France.

However, Cappeau, who was no church loyalist, could not hide his political leanings as a socialist. His distance from the church and involvement in the socialist movement discredited him, as well as the song. Then when church leaders also discovered the composer was a Jew, the Catholic church felt forced to denounce "Cantique de Noel" even though it had become one of the most beloved Christmas songs in France. The lyricist being a socialist and the composer a Jew rendered the song "unfit for church services" with its "total absence of the spirit of religion."

But little did they know...

When the French people would not let this song be buried by the church and kept singing it, an American writer, who was an abolitionist, brought it to the United States, partly because of its focus in the third verse.

> *Truly He taught us to love one another,*
> *His law is love and His gospel is peace.*
> *Chains he shall break, for the slave is our brother.*
> *And in his name all oppression shall cease.*

And the song began to spread in America, even as it continued to be popular on the European continent.

In fact, the story is told of Christmas Eve 1871 during the Franco-Prussian war when one night a French soldier stepped out of his bunker, laid down his rifle and began to sing at the top of his lungs...

*O holy night, the stars are brightly shining.*
*It is the night of our dear Savior's birth.*

In response to this amazing act of bravery and peacemaking, a German soldier stepped out of his bunker and sang the beginning of Luther's Christmas hymn, "Vom Himmel Noch, Da Komm' Ich Her." (From Heaven Above to Earth I Come.) Without political negotiations or cameras rolling, the soldiers simply stopped the war and observed a 24-hour peace in honor of Christmas day.

But little did they know...

On another Christmas Eve 35 years later, some 60 years after Cappeau first penned the words to Cantique de Noel which was later translated by American abolitionist John Sullivan Dwight into the familiar lyrics of O Holy Night, something else incredible happened. Thirty-three year old Reginald Fessenden, the former chief chemist for Thomas Edison, changed the world, when he devised a way to speak into an instrument called a microphone and transmit a wireless signal of a human voice across the airwaves. Up until that point radio operators on sea-going vessels and wireless owners at newspapers heard only *dit-dot-dit-dit* Morse Code transmissions. But on this night they were amazed to hear for the first time in history the sound of a human voice:

*And it came to pass in those days, that there went out a decree from*
*Caesar Augustus, that all the world should be taxed...*

An absolutely incredible miracle!

Then, with the Nativity story read in its entirety, Fessenden picked up his violin and played. He could not have envisioned the scene he had created in many ships and newspaper offices as astonished radio operators called their co-workers to gather round the speakers, listening to the melody of O Holy Night—making it the first-ever music broadcast through the airwaves of planet Earth!

That story remarkably reveals the "little do we know" principle. The priest, the disaffected church-goer turned socialist, the Jew, the American abolitionist, the brave French soldier, and the young scientist experimenting with radio technology had no idea that poem turned beloved Christmas song would have such worldwide impact. All orchestrated by the Lord!

Not only can't we imagine the amazing things God is already up to right now in your life and mine, but there are no restrictions on what He can do and who He can use, or how, or when or where. God is already doing immeasurably more than all we can ask or imagine!

The focus of this final volume of the *Just Ask* series is on learning how to pray confidently about things that are already "in the works" by seeing through the revelation lens of God's Word that they are indeed already in the works. The work of Jesus on the cross inaugurated some never-before-imagined possibilities. But in order to see them we must shed some of the old and limiting ways in which we look at salvation. That's what the next two chapters are about.

# CHAPTER TWO

# The Seed

"Today each one of you is going to begin to grow your own flower," the teacher tells the children in her first grade class. She holds up a small Dixie cup with an orange marigold standing erect. The kids respond in the way they have for generations in every city and small town school ever built—with a perfectly synchronous, "Ooooooooh," that rises and falls as if floating along the curve of a sine wave.

She continues to explain, "Each one of you will have a cup like this one"—she gestures like a magician—"which you will fill with two inches of fresh dirt." She emphasizes the word *fresh*, and then she pinches a small seed on her desk and lifts it forward toward the class to give each student a better look.

"Then you will take one small seed just like this one and place it in the dirt and push it gently under the soil."

She does just that in front of their wide eyes and continues, "Finally we'll take a little bit of water and sprinkle it on the dirt. Not too much..." She dramatizes the warning with her voice, "...or else the seed will drown and die before it can grow into a beyooooootiful flower."

Hands shoot up all around the class room, each student asking the same question, "How long before the flower grows?"

The teacher knows that question is coming. After all that is a big part of the reason for doing this exercise. It's always been the reason. "You're going to have to be patient and wait. It won't happen as fast as you want. But it will happen," she reassures the kids.

"But how long?

"A whole hour?"

"A day?

"Will we have flowers when we come back in the morning?"

"No, it will take longer than that." She breaks the bad news. "It will be at least a whole week before you even see anything come up through the dirt. Even then it will be very tiny and you will have to look very carefully. But don't be mistaken, there will be a lot happening below the soil that you can't see."

Now that the teacher has their full attention she begins to tell them how every seed has three parts: the embryo—"That's the part that you will actually see come up through the soil"; the endosperm— "That's the big package of food the embryo eats to grow big and strong enough to push it's way up through the soil"; the husk— "That's like the wrapping of a Christmas gift that has to be torn open to get to the gift inside."

All this time the children never take their eyes off the teacher or the flower she holds before them. So she pauses to take a breath, to move the mood from wonder to gravity.

"You see, children, what has to happen in order for this beautiful flower to appear is this: The seed actually has to die. I don't want you to be sad about that, but you need to know that flowers teach us a very important lesson. The tiny flower has to leave the seed behind in order to become a full-grown flower. This is an important lesson we'll learn by watching our flowers grow."

Probably each one of us has had a school experience just like that. Nevertheless somehow we forget the lesson, at least as it applies in other areas of life. And it does apply almost always. To become an adult you have to let go of childhood dependencies and strike out on your own. To have the joy of parenthood you have to let go of the footloose days of marriage when you could do almost anything you want at a moment's notice. To have the incredible second-chance joy of grandchildren you have to pack up your kids and drop them off at their adult life way too soon and drive away.

Every stage of our growth requires the dying of some seed, some husk of protection we'd like to retain, some kind of familiar structure or container of security that holds things together.

If that is the way God designed the flow of life and growth, might it not also be true of God's life-giving salvation? Is it possible that God's plan of salvation came into the world as a seed? Are there ways in which He first introduced, described and provided salvation that must be shed before we can see and experience full salvation?

I believe the answer is yes, and this chapter is my support for that claim, which sets us on the path for the rest of this book.

## A VALID ANALOGY

Before we make too much out of the seed analogy we must be sure it is proper to do so from a biblical point of view. Analogies are helpful ways to create understanding, but they have to be validated by scripture.

We don't have to look too hard in scripture to recognize God actually elevates the analogy of the seed process to a position of fundamental importance. There are many places in scripture that support this conclusion, but one from the Old Testament and two from the New Testament are all we need to claim this analogy has deep roots in the Bible.

Is it possible that God's plan of salvation came into the world as a seed?

In Isaiah 55 the Lord uses the image of the seed to analogize the production of spiritual food on earth, as His spoken words shower the earth with His ways and thoughts.

> *As the rain and the snow come down from heaven, and do not return to it without watering the earth and making it bud and flourish, so that it yields seed for the sower and bread for the eater, so is my word that goes out from my mouth: It will not return to me*

*empty, but will accomplish what I desire and achieve the purpose*
*for which I sent it.*   Isaiah 55:10-11

Then in the New Testament Jesus uses the seed analogy in the famous parable of the sower. Here the *seed process* is explicitly emphasized by virtue of the contrasted elements of the parable: the trodden path, the rocky places with shallow soil, the thorn-infested areas and the good soil. In each case the issue is whether the seed could complete its process of yielding an abundant harvest.

*"Listen! A farmer went out to sow his seed. As he was scattering the*
*seed, some fell along the path, and the birds came and ate it up.*
*Some fell on rocky places, where it did not have much soil. It sprang*
*up quickly, because the soil was shallow. But when the sun came*
*up, the plants were scorched, and they withered because they had no*
*root. Other seed fell among thorns, which grew up and choked the*
*plants, so that they did not bear grain. Still other seed fell on good*
*soil. It came up, grew and produced a crop, multiplying thirty, sixty,*
*or even a hundred times."*   Mark 4:3-8

Jesus point? Whether it is pecking birds or scorching sun or choking weeds, if anything interrupts the seed process abundant growth and harvest will not occur.

In Matthew's gospel, immediately following the parable of the sower, Jesus tells another parable featuring a tiny mustard seed that is able to complete its process and becomes something altogether new and glorious: a huge sanctuarial tree representing the spreading kingdom.

*He told them another parable: "The kingdom of heaven is like a*
*mustard seed, which a man took and planted in his field. Though*
*it is the smallest of all your seeds, yet when it grows, it is the largest*
*of garden plants and becomes a tree, so that the birds of the air come*
*and perch in its branches."*   Matthew 13:31-32

The analogy of the seed is fundamental, including then the seed process as an illustrative part of the way God does His work.

## UNLESS THE SEED DIES

That seed process is just what the teacher explains to her first-grade students. The seed must die. That death occurs in three stages. Something must activate the beginning of the germination process, usually the application of water. The dormant embryo inside begins to devour the nourishing endosperm and then breaks through the husk, which falls away and fertilizes the emerging plant. Even though all the genetic material of the final plant is contained in the embryo, what comes into being is altogether new and vastly different than the seed.

As you read those words please consider them in light of two statements in the New Testament:

> *Jesus replied, "I tell you the truth, unless a kernel of wheat falls to the ground and dies, it remains only a single seed. But if it dies, it produces many seeds.*  John 12:24

> *Therefore if any man be in Christ, he is a new creature: old things are passed away; behold, all things are become new.*
> 2 Corinthians 5:17 (KJV)

There is no way around this seed process. It is God's design. Before something altogether new can take place, something must be left behind. Something must be shed, discarded, or renounced. Let's take a look at another case in point found in one of the scriptures we already highlighted.

In Isaiah 55 we read about God's ways being higher than our ways and His thoughts being higher than our thoughts. But the point of that chapter is not to warn us to stay humble in the light of His greatness and "otherness." As I pointed out in *Just Ask, Volume One* (page 72) the context of that statement is a chapter with the theme of invitation—invitation to get something from God we absolutely need but are too poor to purchase. His ways and thoughts are unreachably beyond us, but that's why He sends His ways and thoughts to earth in the form of His spoken words. This is a remarkable promise, not

Before something altogether new can take place, something must be left behind. Something must be shed, discarded, or renounced.

a theological warning. We can actually have a harvest of God's wisdom growing in our lives through divine revelation. But there is a preliminary requirement: We must shed our own ways and thoughts to make room for His to take root and grow to harvest.

> *Seek the Lord while he may be found; call on him while he is near.*
> *Let the wicked **forsake his way** and the evil man his thoughts.*
>
> Isaiah 55:6-7

This is the prerequisite for having a harvest of divine wisdom and revelation. We must let our ways and thoughts die. We must leave them behind. Renounce them in favor of having them replaced by ways and thoughts that are far greater, that only come through gracious, divine delivery.

By now this principle is probably beginning to ring a bell. You're thinking, *Of course, this is what I have known all along. You have to die to yourself in order to have eternal life. You have to surrender, to repent.*

You're right. This seed process is all through the Bible. And the ultimate example of this principle is Jesus Himself, who died, shed His mortal body and rose with an immortal body. Of course.

But as familiar and obvious as this now sounds, the point of this chapter is to urge you to apply this to what we imagine salvation to hold for us.

Here's the problem. When we think of salvation we think of God fixing and restoring what once was his perfect design. However, as I said in the previous chapter, salvation is not only about Him correcting something old and broken but of Him creating some brand new, never-before-imagined realities.

Salvation must be ushering in something entirely better than ever before, not just something repaired or essentially the same but slightly improved.

The author of Hebrews spends several chapters trying to get this across to His readers who were steeped in Jewish traditions. They did not seem to understand that Christianity is not just improved Judaism; it is a brand new religion that

Salvation must be ushering in something entirely better than ever before, not just something repaired or essentially the same but slightly improved.

requires shedding the husk of Judaism. He is urging them to recognize that the new covenant is not just a way of making the old covenant work better. The new covenant ushers in a completely new order that offers what was never before possible. We need to unpack this. Then we will see why this is so important as it pertains to salvation and prayer.

## SHEDDING JUDAISM

Over the years I have appreciated several parishioners who adhere closely to Old Testament observances. They sincerely observe Jewish feasts and rituals, and find in them deep meaning and enhancements for rich devotional lives. While they never judge or criticize those who don't share their beliefs, they wish that all Christians would follow the Old Testament patterns of worship religiously. I don't doubt their allegiance to Jesus (or Yeshua as they prefer), nor do I doubt their understanding of salvation by faith not by works. They are, to coin a term, Messianic Evangelicals. So their observance of the law is properly valued as a means of grace, not a requirement for salvation.

However, I have never found it necessary to go as far as they do in my religious practices. I find their detailed knowledge of the Old Testament symbolism to be a valuable aid to understanding many of Jesus' words and much of the New Testament. But I find it very difficult to promote or engage in such a strong embrace of Old Testament traditions when the writer to the Hebrews (and other places in scripture) clearly calls his readers to leave their allegiance to the old covenant behind, at least in terms of its practice and value. In fact, he refers to that covenant and its practices as "obsolete" (Hebrews 8:13). That is a strong word that denotes something that no longer serves us well in light of something newer and much better. Let's note a few of the places the writer makes this clear:

> *The former regulation is **set aside** because it was **weak and useless** (for the law made nothing perfect), and a better hope is introduced, by which we draw near to God.* Hebrews 7:18-19

> The new covenant is not just a way of making the old covenant work better. The new covenant ushers in a completely new order that offers what was never before possible.

*Jesus has become the guarantee of a **better covenant.** Because Jesus lives forever, he has a permanent priesthood. Therefore he is able to save completely those who come to God through him, because he always lives to intercede for them.* Hebrews 7:24-25

*The ministry Jesus has received is as **superior** to theirs as the covenant of which he is mediator **is superior to the old one,** and it is founded on better promises. For if there had been nothing **wrong with that first covenant,** no place would have been sought for another.* Hebrews 8:6-7

*Now the first covenant had regulations for worship and also an earthly sanctuary. ...This is an illustration for the present time, indicating that the gifts and sacrifices being offered were **not able** to clear the conscience of the worshiper. They are only a matter of food and drink and various ceremonial washings—external regulations **applying until the time of the new order.*** Hebrews 9:1, 9-10

*The law is **only a shadow** of the good things that are coming—**not the realities themselves.** For this reason it can never, by the same sacrifices repeated endlessly year after year, make perfect those who draw near to worship. If it could, would they not have stopped being offered?* Hebrews 10:1-2

These are just a few snippets lifted from the author's extended argument that the old covenant along with all its trappings must necessarily be set aside, because their effects are temporary and inferior to the effects of the works of Jesus Christ in the new covenant. Because of who He is, no priestly works or tabernacle rituals need ever be practiced again, and we now have something so much better than ever before.

Again, I hasten to add that Old Testament practices have rich meaning—meaning worth understanding and applying as we seek to understand scripture and enrich our appreciation of God's grace shown in Christ Jesus. However, my spirit recoils from giving the Old Testament practices too much regard and enthusiasm in favor of reserving my fervor for what the new covenant now makes possible that was never before possible: a new heart made perfect in love, direct access to God, and a totally relieved conscience. That's what I get excited about. That's the feast I invite people to observe and enter.

But even if the old covenant is obsolete, should we not continue to promote the observance of those patterns as devotional steps for drawing closer to God and remaining in right relationship to Him?

I don't think that's necessary. The New Testament reveals that Gentiles *did not* have to understand the Old Testament practices in order to fully experience the New Testament realities. In fact, when we do find the Old Testament practices elucidated in the pages of the New Testament it is mostly when Jewish people were having a hard time fully embracing the realities of the new covenant. It seems that New Testament writers had to explain Jesus in Old Testament terms in order to get them to open their ears to the New Testament claims. It was not because people couldn't enter fully into the new order without going through the portal of old covenant practices and symbolism.

## IN WITH THE NEW

In short, the seed process—that is, the old must die away—applies to a full experience of new covenant realities. There are elements of the Old Testament way of perceiving and practicing faith that must be shed in order for a person to experience the realities of this new covenant. That's what the writer to the Hebrews is saying. Indeed his words are only an echo of what Jesus was also trying to say when he taught his largely Jewish listeners. Let's examine a few of the Old Testament ways of thinking that must be shed in favor of the brand new, never-before-imagined experience of salvation.

There are elements of the Old Testament way of perceiving and practicing faith that must be shed in order for a person to experience the realities of this new covenant.

### *OLD: The presence of God is maintained through avoiding contamination.*

That is what was drummed into the minds of God's people from the moment they were led out of Egypt. Don't touch! Don't touch anything dead. Don't touch anything unclean. Don't touch lepers. Secretions of every sort make you unclean.

### *NEW: The presence of God is ministered as we touch what is contaminated.*

When Jesus ushered in the kingdom of God He brought a new order of righteousness. It was not about avoiding, but anointing. It was not about maintaining God's presence through avoiding contact with anything unclean, but about ministering God's presence and cleansing toward what you touch. So Jesus touched a leper before he healed him (Matthew 8:3). He touched a dead girl to raise her to life (Mark 5:41). He secreted spit in the dirt, stirred it with his fingers and anointed a man's blind eyes to give him sight (John 9:6).

How did that shift occur? Does God no longer care about holiness, about clean hands and clean hearts? Yes, He does. But He cares more about rescuing people, so He provides permanent spiritual cleansing and imparts a covering of the spotless righteousness of Jesus to every believer. Thus He maintains His presence for us—we don't have to do that—so that we can impart His presence to others in peace, healing and wisdom.

This Old Testament impulse to take on ourselves the task of avoiding contamination must be shed; we must trust Jesus' righteousness. Or else, we become separatists who avoid contact with the very people Jesus wants us to love and rescue. That seed must die. God wants a new, never-before-imagined company of followers who are so thoroughly made holy that we are impervious to the disqualification of sin and paralysis of shame.

### *OLD: The priestly and prophetic roles are reserved for a special class of people.*

In the Old Covenant people were assigned roles and tasks that were vigorously

protected. Any crossing over into another role was a punishable trespass. Only priests could pronounce forgiveness and intercede for sinful people. Only priests could impart covenant blessings or carry the needs of people into the presence of God.

Only a specially called and anointed person—a prophet—could speak on God's behalf and accurately predict future events. Many people tried to appoint themselves to that role, but they were false prophets. Their future predictions did not come true. Their messages were lies created to tell people what they wanted to hear.

### NEW: All believers become eligible to function as priests and prophets.

Young men. Old men. Even women and servants. That new order was ushered in on the day of Pentecost, according to the apostle Peter, who explained that the supernatural phenomena being manifested was the fulfillment of Joel's prophecy.

> *"In the last days, God says, I will pour out my Spirit on all people. Your sons and daughters will prophesy, your young men will see visions, your old men will dream dreams. Even on my servants, both men and women, I will pour out my Spirit in those days, and they will prophesy."*

Acts 2:17-18

Since the day of Pentecost any follower of Jesus can function prophetically. Any believer may from time to time be anointed situationally with the spiritual gift of prophecy, enabled in that moment by the Spirit of God to speak words of proclamation or even prediction. It now is possible for any believer to experience what was the norm for Jesus:

> *For I did not speak of my own accord, but the Father who sent me commanded me what to say and how to say it.* John 12:49

Additionally, we are the fulfillment of God's words to Moses that God was creating a kingdom of priests. Peter affirmed that when he called the members of the church "a royal priesthood" (1 Peter 2:9). As priests we can enter directly into God's presence, we can receive God's forgiveness and cleansing, and we can actually pronounce blessing and forgiveness in Jesus' name.

### OLD: Devotion is expressed through ritualistic disciplines.

You can't read through Exodus, Leviticus and Numbers without getting the message: The Old Covenant is all about keeping the rules. If you fear God you will revere His laws; if you belong to Him and Him alone you will follow His decrees to the letter. Those who are devoted to God walk in His holy ways.

### NEW: Devotion is expressed through bold, productive use of the resources of the Master.

Things changed drastically in the new covenant. His ways are still holy, but they are not ritualistic. Yes, in some cases the church's advice was to avoid eating meat offered to idols (Acts 15:20). But even that was not a huge deal to Paul. It was more of a concession to people of weak faith, because now there is a reversal. Things you touch don't make you unholy. Rather, things you touch are made holy, if indeed the Holy Spirit is in you.

This reversal was shocking to Paul's readers, and still is to us today. For example, Paul tells us that meat sacrificed to idols is rendered harmless and can be holy and glorifying to God when we eat it with thanksgiving to God (Romans 14:14, 1 Corinthians 10:27). And more shockingly, unbelieving spouses are sanctified by their believing mates (2 Corinthians 7:14).

Consequently, devotion to God is no longer primarily expressed through following holiness rules rigorously, although there are still rules of course. Now, in the new order of the kingdom, devotion is expressed through bold, productive use of the resources of the Master. If you really revere the Master, you will make as much use of what He gives you as possible. That is the message of Jesus' foundational Parable of the Talents (Luke 19:12-27). The faithful and devoted servants are the ones who steward the Master's resources to a place of increase.

Also according to Jesus, among the resources He gives is the outpouring of divinely inspired words flowing through you in prayer. Jesus promised if you use His words in prayer, you will bear much fruit, which brings glory to God and shows that you are a devoted follower of His (John 15:7-8).

Do you see how this new covenant provides a totally new way of living? In just these three examples (and in coming chapters we will explore more) we see a radical new form of righteous devotion. It's about receiving and trusting the holy presence of God in us to such a degree that we engage in His work with confidence and without reluctance in spite of our own inadequacies.

> Righteous devotion is about receiving and trusting the holy presence of God in us to such a degree that we engage in His work with confidence and without reluctance in spite of our own inadequacies.

I have a graphic and humbling personal story that illustrates this new covenant possibility, but I need to appeal to your grace and spirit of forgiveness before you read it. Can you offer me that? What I am about to share is my most personal but foundational testimony, which reveals how I can be so certain about the new covenant possibilities. But it may be a hard testimony for some people to hear...

Ever since I was a young teen, before I had any say in the matter—or so it seemed—I had a strong and perverse sexual desire that overtook and overwhelmed me from time to time. I was the typical "good Christian kid" from a "good Christian home" so I was disgusted by my desire and the choices I made. I fought against this desire and was largely successful most of the time. But just when I thought "it" was gone and wouldn't come back, it did. My problem continued on through high school and college. Then... on into marriage.

I was married to the most beautiful girl in the world in my estimation, and our relationship was about as healthy as any young marriage can be—which means we still had a long way to go to learn to love each other unconditionally and unselfishly. And we had a satisfying sexual relationship too. But none of that erased my problem.

In our second year of marriage, I was a youth director in an upstanding city church and my wife was a school teacher in a fledgling Christian school meeting in the basement of another church. We were a typical young couple with one car, so our routine involved me dropping her off at school in the morning and picking her up in the late afternoon.

One day after dropping her off, after a long season of walking the "straight and narrow," my problem hi-jacked my morning. I was unprepared and fell again to my sin.

By noon it was over. I was crushed. But by the time I picked up Margie at school I had already gone through my all-too-familiar ritual of sorrow and heartfelt confession to the Lord, so I could plaster the "all is well" look on my face when she got in the car.

Little did I know that this day would be different. All would *not* be well.

We were driving home from her school, only about five blocks from our house, when two police cars came out of nowhere and pulled us over. Within seconds I was arrested, placed in the back of one of their cars, and Margie was told to follow them in our car. She was completely in the dark, and still today I can only imagine what it must have been like for her. The earthquake!

At the police station I was questioned, confronted and threatened, even though I readily confessed. For a few moments I was left alone in an interrogation room, and in those moments I imagined my whole life ending. Losing everything.

I could have lost everything, and most probably would have if this had happened today rather than in 1976. But for some reason the detectives saw something in me that moved them to extend mercy. I didn't ask for it. But they offered.

Rather than charge me with my crime, they offered the offended party five minutes to shame and punish me verbally as loudly and angrily as they wanted. Of course I deserved that and more. But my life was not ruined and everything I now have in my life and have done in my life is owing to the gift of mercy I was shown in that moment.

When I was released and saw Margie for the first time, my depth of shame, embarassment and sorrow could not be expressed. Not even sobs of tears could say what I wished I could have said to Margie to heal how I had broken her heart and her world.

It took several years before we could even begin to talk about that day and my problem. Even as I write this now and even though that problem was soon arrested by a powerful work of the Holy Spirit and I have lived for more than 35 years free of that perverted sexual desire, I am surprised and yet not too surprised that my sorrow over the pain I caused my wife is still close to the surface. This is true even though she has long since forgiven me and lives out that forgiveness with a continual gift of trust.

Here's the point of my sharing that testimony. It's not to proclaim the power of God to thoroughly deliver a person from the most powerful urges of sexual sin—although that is true and is a bedrock element of my faith and ministry. Here's why I share this testimony in this chapter.

During that time in the midst of my problem, I was engaged in what has proven to be one of the most fruitful evangelistic seasons of my ministry! Even with this secret sin, a sin that was also a crime, even though I was spoiled goods, contaminated and broken by my own filthy behavior, somehow because of the new covenant, because of the new order inaugurated by the death and resurrection of Jesus Christ, because His sacrifice was offered once for all, and because His righteousness clothed me, when I shared the gospel with teenagers in my youth group, they said yes to Jesus.

I had more people respond to my invitations to salvation in those two years than in any other season of my ministry. And what's more, their responses were genuine. They have been faithful to the Lord ever since, some even going into full-time Christian service.

Please don't take this testimony the wrong way. I am certainly not saying that sin doesn't matter, nor that we shouldn't have a passion for holiness that moves us desperately toward purity in behavior and speech. But I am saying that through God's salvation and the new covenant everything changed.

Through the sacrifice of Jesus Christ we believers now have a powerful and permanent righteousness that keeps us in a constant state of divine acceptance, provides the continous blessing of divine presence, and qualifies us for divine usefulness even while we are in process of learning obedience, rooting out pockets of sin and growing in righteousness.

This is the new order.

If a person grasps this new, never-before-imagined opportunity for righteousness and fruitfulness in spite of our own brokenness, he or she will live in a brand new place of confidence and boldness.

One of the Enemy's most effective methods to hamstring God's people is to keep feeding you the old covenant assumption that you have to be holy by your own efforts before you can come into God's presence and be useful. So all the Enemy has to do is to call your attention to your flaws and needle you over your failures, and he winds up stiffling your sense of freedom in Christ and fitness for service.

The old covenant is about who you are and what you've done. The new covenant is about who Christ is and what He's done.

The Old Covenant was a seed for the germination of the New Covenant. Salvation does not simply restore what was lost and repair what was broken. It replaces something inferior and inadequate with something incredible.

Let the old seed die, so that the new possibilities can occur.

Some of the new possibilities are so incredible they deserve a whole chapter to themselves. That's where we are headed. However, we still have one more exercise in shifting our way of thinking in order to prepare for understanding and embracing the forward-looking view of salvation. Therefore, in the next chapter we will see how the environment in which we hammer out our theology controls what we imagine as possible.

Illustration by Kyle T. Webster

# CHAPTER THREE

# Wilderness

"Oh! But he was a tight-fisted hand at the grindstone, Scrooge. A squeezing, wrenching, grasping, scraping, clutching, covetous old sinner! Hard and sharp as flint, from which no steel had ever struck out generous fire; secret, and self-contained, and solitary as an oyster."

That's the famous description of Ebeneezer Scrooge in Stave One of Charles Dickens' *A Christmas Carol.*

Dickens was perhaps unknowingly a pioneer of psychoanalysis. He did not have the benefit of reading the work of Sigmund Freud. But his beloved story, with its use of the three ghosts of Christmas, takes us into territory that parallels the analyst's couch as it unpacks the traumas of Scrooge's past, the fears of his future and how they conspired to create a present day cynicism in stark contrast to the gentle-hearted gratefulness of the Cratchit family.

In effect, Dickens attempted to answer the question, What made

Scrooge Scrooge? What shaped his outloook on life? In Stave Two the Ghost of Christmas Past takes us to several vantage points and allows us to peer into scenes that show us that he was motherless, being raised by a cruel father, sent off to boarding school, neglected at Christmastime, and racked with fear of poverty that led him to choose money over a loving fiancé who broke their engagement with these words:

> *"You fear the world too much," she answered, gently. "All your other hopes have merged into the hope of being beyond the chance of its sordid reproach. I have seen your nobler aspirations fall off one by one, until the master-passion, Gain, engrosses you. Have I not?"*

Dickens does not tell us exactly *when* or *how*, but shows us *that* Scrooge had adopted a view of life corresponding with an increasingly popular philosophy of his day that valued hard work and wealth, and ascribed blame to the poor for their lowly condition.

Dickens was spot on regarding the power of the past to shape the attitude of the mind, the values and perceptions of life a person comes to adopt. People who study such things talk about the "long shadow" various forms of abuse cast across a person's life well into their adulthood. Without help they may never come out from under that shadow.

Young children who grow up with cold fathers may never fully connect with the fatherhood of God. Indeed, some don't even want to. Because of their upbringing it is a useless metaphor.

What is true of individuals is also true of whole people groups. My wife and I were once asked to come to a country in eastern Europe to do some teaching on marriage relationships.

"What is it you hope to accomplish through the course of our days together?" we asked the seminar coordinator.

He said, "All of the young couples grew up under communism. They have never known anything else. In communistic countries you are never sure who is watching, whether they will report you for something. They've never known what it means to have relationships based on trust. Actually they can't imagine what that is like and how to foster them. Try to help them see what a trusting relationship can be like."

The environment of a person's upbringing shapes not only the individual's but a whole society's outlook. In this chapter I plan to show you how the same principle affects the way we develop and affirm our theological outlook. But first...

❦

Imagine this hypothetical experiment. Create two groups of 10,000 people each. Have them watch ½ hour of national and global news, then ½ hour of local news every day for one year. Have Group A watch broadcasts that are ninety percent bad news (murder, mayhem, scandal, geopolitical unrest, crises, natural disasters, fires, explosions, corporate greed, political corruption, economic instability, job losses, traffic accidents, market crashes and sundry other crimes and tragedies) and ten percent good news (commendable achievements, human interest stories, human kindness, etc.).

*The environment of a person's upbringing shapes not only the individual's but a whole society's outlook.*

Have Group B watch broadcasts that are the reverse of Group A: ninety percent good news and ten percent bad news. At the end of one year administer an exam that assesses each person's outlook on life.

Do we even need to conduct this experiment in order to predict the results? Probably not. We would anticipate that Group A would have a more pessimistic outlook than Group B. Probably by a large degree.

But here's the more significant point. Probably Group A would argue vehemently that they were not being pessimistic, but simply realistic. In other words, they would argue "that's the way things are."

To be sure, every news report they heard would have been true and accurate taken individually. However, they would be guilty of the logical fallacy known as "begging the question." To take in all the "evidence" without realizing that their observations were limited to bad news and conclude that those observations accurately described "the way things are" is jumping to conclusions.

They are assuming the truth of the very thing yet to be proved. That's "question begging." They are assuming that the ratio between good and bad news was accurately represented by the news programs they watched. But how would they know that?

Simply put, if every night they watch news about two murders, five break-ins, two car accidents, one house fire, they are forgetting that in a city of one million people, 400,000 homes, and 750,000 vehicles that means there were 999,998 people who were not murdered, 749,998 cars not in an accident, and 399,999 homes that did not burn.

*Our theology of salvation cannot and must not be shaped by previous or present experience only but primarily by **promised** experience.*

This calls into question whether the people in Group A have a clearer grasp of reality than those in Group B. Which group is truly more realistic in their outlook and expectations? Group B. Those whose diet of news is closer to the accurate ratio of the experiences of most people will have a more accurate view of reality.

If that is the case—since it is unquestionably the case that one's news and information diet affects his or her perception of reality—I would suggest that the observations presented by one's environment will also shape one's theology. For a theology is nothing more than a formal articulation of one's view of reality as it pertains to God in relation to His creation, His will and His ways among people.

In this volume of the *Just Ask* series we are asking what salvation looks like as we focus forward on what was not-yet imagined or experienced by people before the time of the cross. What was God wanting to create, not just correct? Therefore our theology of salvation—that is, what has salvation made possible?—cannot and must not be shaped by previous or present experience only but primarily by *promised* experience.

And yet, if I am correct in my observations, our theologies tend to be written in the context of previous and present experiences only. If it seems God promises one thing, but our experiences do not corroborate that, then we write our theology excluding any confidence in that promise. For example, if God promises that through salvation we will do the same things Jesus did and in greater measure but our experience does not bear witness to that fact, then we exclude that expectation from our theology. What's more, we not only exclude it, but sadly we marshal our theological powers to explain it away!

As long as we are doing hypothetical experiments, let's imagine another.

## A WILDERNESS SEMINARY

Imagine for a moment that some Israelites approached Moses during the wilderness period of Jewish history and proposed the creation of a seminary:

*"Ever since we were released from bondage in Egypt we have had a few experiences with God. Now here we are in the desert wandering and waiting to enter the Promised Land some day. Some of us are dying. New generations are coming along, but they know nothing of the exodus. We can tell them stories, but what do our experiences tell us about God that is true for all time. Frankly, we are not sure what to say. Sometimes God seems one way; sometimes another. We need to appoint some of our best thinkers to come up with a systematic way of articulating what we believe so that we can pass it on to our children. We propose the formation of a theological seminary."*

If they had done this, what would their theology have been? What would they have taught their young people? How would they have described the nature of a relationship with God? How would they have defined sin? And since all theology inevitably creates windows into possibilities, what would their expectations have been about their lives in relationship to God?

Think of the experiences that would have shaped their theology, their view of God, their view of life, their view of promises. Up to this point they had known God's miraculous provision of food. It was an ongoing blessing, but a blessing they had long since interpreted as a burdensome routine, a monotonous menu. It is not hard to imagine their theological catechism including an article like this:

*Article #8: To say that God is our Provider entails His commitment to provide us with our daily mimimum requirements for survival.*

Then on top of that, they would have recalled their experiences when they asked God for a better diet. "We were tired of the taste of manna and the boring routine of gathering it. All we did was share our feelings of frustration and ask God for something different, something to excite our palate for once. And the next thing we knew, we're getting quail stuffed down our throats that made us sick to our stomach. Some of us died!"

In light of that experience the theologians might have written the following article of faith:

> *Article #15: Staying in a right relationship with God requires*
> *a willingness to set aside any desire for special pleasures.*

In addition to these experiences with God as their Provider, their sojourn in the wilderness involved many experiences of punishment and forfeiture. Yes, they enjoyed several experiences of miraculous deliverance, guidance and provision. But those experiences were more than counterbalanced by demonstrations of His anger and judgment. Can you imagine the theologians trying to hammer out a statement about the nature of God based on those experiences? The resulting article might have read something like this:

> *Article #5: While it is true God can be merciful and gracious,*
> *His moods and actions are unpredictable. He is just as likely*
> *to be stern and impatient.*

It's not hard to imagine something like that becoming their theology of the nature of God due to their experiences with Him. Then couple that with the intricately detailed nature of His commands governing everything from skin eruptions to carcass disposal, from offerings to offal, including the stern warnings against minute violations. The theologians might have penned this:

> *Article #16: The holiness required of His people to stay in right*
> *relationship with a holy God involves meticulous adherence*
> *to every ritual and rule.*

Just in case you question the theological propositions I imagine coming from this hypothetical wilderness seminary, bear in mind that my proof is in the pudding of the Pharisees. It seems beyond argument that the Pharisees of Jesus' day were living within the framework of this—let's call it—*wilderness theology.*

They had become exactly like the God in this imagined wilderness theology. Stern. Impatient. Unmerciful. Jot-and-tittle-y.

Now imagine a young upstart theologian standing in a seminary class proposing a different view of God. She says, "The nature of God is to bless His people beyond anything they can imagine. He provides abundantly. He fills their lives with good things. He loves them like the best father anyone could ever imagine."

How would her words be received? She would be ridiculed. The theologians would say her viewpoint is not borne out by their experience or nascent traditions.

"Be reasonable," they would urge with a measure of condescension. "You may be basing your assumptions on some of God's words; that's true. He did make some promises about bringing us into a land of milk and honey, and the like. But how can we take that literally when so much of what we are experiencing points in another direction? We must shape our theology realistically. God's words are at best metaphorical, and therefore, they provide no sure ground for theological propositions."

On the one hand what I just wrote is imagined. On the other it is essentially what Jesus faced when He tried to introduce the theologians of His day to a different view of God. He told them about a heavenly Father who wanted to welcome sinners back into His arms, rather than avoid or condemn them as the Pharisees did. He showed them the blessing nature of God through unbridled acts of healing and abundant provision. He showed them that all the rules were made for man's good not man for the rules. This was a theology they could not accept, because it was trumped by the one based on their wilderness experience, rather than God's word.

It seems beyond argument that the Pharisees of Jesus' day were living within the framework of this wilderness theology.

Like the Group A people in our news experiment, they could not think outside the confines of their experience-based assumptions about the nature of God and reality.

The problem with doing theology in the wilderness, of course, is that you have to be very careful not to forget that the so-called "realities" are what they are because of disobedience, distrust and a worldly disposition, not God's nature or His will or ways.

Now imagine the formation of another seminary in a completely different environment. Rather than originating in the wilderness period, what if the seminary were formed in the Promised Land during a season of God's promised *shalom*? How would the theology be different?

## PROMISED LAND SEMINARY

Imagine something called the Promised Land Seminary. Imagine it is formed after a whole generation of people experienced exactly what God had promised before the people entered the land. Of course, that didn't actually happen. There never was a time when God's people experienced fully what God had promised, because their obedience and trust was also sporadic, like their predecessors. But imagine they had obeyed and thus enjoyed all the Promised Land held in store for them. Then imagine them wanting to set up a seminary to shape an accurate theology for future generations. What would their professors teach?

To figure that out we only need to look at what God promised as recorded in Deuteronomy (similar promises are also found in Leviticus 26) before the people went into the Promised Land. Those promises coalesced into three primary categories:

**Prosperity and abundance:**

*The fruit of your womb will be blessed, and the crops of your land and the young of your livestock—the calves of your herds and the lambs of your flocks. Your basket and your kneading trough will be blessed. You will be blessed when you come in and blessed when you go out... The Lord will send a blessing on your barns and on everything you put your hand to. The Lord will grant you abundant prosperity—in the fruit of your womb, the young of your livestock and the crops of your ground—in the land he swore to your forefathers to give you. The Lord will open the heavens, the storehouse of his bounty, to send rain on your land in season and to bless all the work of your hands.* Deuteronomy 28:4-6,8, 11-12

**Supremacy and glory:**

*The Lord your God will set you high above all the nations on earth. The Lord will grant that the enemies who rise up against you will be defeated before you. They will come at you from one direction but flee from you in seven. Then all the peoples on earth will see that you are called by the name of the Lord, and they will fear you. You will lend to many nations but will borrow from none. The Lord will make you the head, not the tail.* Deuteronomy 28:1,7,10,13

**Holiness and devotion:**

*The Lord will establish you as his holy people... The Lord your God will circumcise your hearts and the hearts of your descendants, so that you may love him with all your heart and with all your soul, and live.* Deuteronomy 28:9; 30:6

Put all these features of the Promised Land together and you have what the Bible calls shalom: absolute peace, wholeness, right order, harmony, tranquility and security all brought about and guaranteed by God's enveloping presence.

Now imagine growing up in that shalom environment. You've never known anything else or less. You're now a scholar who is on faculty at Promised Land Seminary with colleagues who have grown up just like you, and you all are being asked to write a theology for future generations. What will your theology teach about the nature of God, His will and His ways? It will be markedly different and much more optimistic than the theology coming out of Wilderness Seminary. Its articles of the faith will include basic assumptions about God's goodness, His prodigious love, His faithful and fervent protection, and His exaltation of His people above any threatening power or opponent.

## CHOOSE YOUR THEOLOGY WISELY

The question is which theology would be the true theology? It would be the one that was written in the context of experiencing all that was possible in a relationship with God. It would not be the theology written in an environment of lack and shortfall.

Here's my argument. We must make sure our contemporary theology is being written based on the Word of God and any experiences of fulfilled divine promises, even if those are not our personal experiences. Unfortunately, this is often not the case. Too often we let our "wilderness" context—an environment of lack—provide the raw data for constructing our theology.

So for example, let's take the theological issue of spiritual gifts. Today many Christians reject the idea that supernatural spiritual gifts, like healing, prophecy, words of knowledge and tongues still exist. Or if they acknowledge their possible existence, they relegate them to a special category of gifts that occur only under exceptional and infrequent conditions: say, on mission fields as a burst of divine power to give witch doctors their come-uppins.

Then with a theology that effectively rules out the supernatural dimension of the spiritual gifts, it becomes necessary to redefine the idea of spiritual gifts and create a theology that "natural-izes" (and neutralizes) divine gifts by placing them safely on spiritual gift inventories along with a host of other non-supernatural, God-given abilities. We do this even though an honest reading of God's Word clearly categorizes the gifts of the Spirit as *supernatural* manifestations, not *natural* God-given abilities.

Why do we do this? Because ultimately we are writing our theology in a wilderness context. Most of our mainstream evangelical churches do not teach or allow for the operation of the supernatural spiritual gifts. Consequently, supernatural spiritual gifts are not commonly experienced, and therefore we don't incorporate them into our theology.

That is why, when we do theology, we should do our thinking with both feet planted in God's Word and not reject something that the Bible clearly affirms until we have traveled the world of other Christians' experiences to find any other context where the Word of God is being corroborated on those issues.

Too often we let our "wilderness" context— an environment of lack—provide the raw data for constructing our theology.

For most of us that means traveling outside our theological context into arenas where people claim to function in the supernatural gifts. We can do that these days by hopping on the internet and searching for verified and validated ministries where these gifts are being experienced and explained. This will likely mean researching countries where the culture is not overrun with western decadence and deadening intellectualism that always quenches the flowing of God's Spirit.

Western decadence and deadening intellectualism always quenches the flowing of God's Spirit.

Spiritual gifts are just one example. The problem of wilderness theology manifests itself in many other areas of faith and life. What kind of divine intervention do we expect from God in matters like financial hardship, marital strife, common depression, career decisions or physical problems? Too many Christians, having been raised with a wilderness theology, expect very little divine assistance in these cases and turn instead to any other form of help they find through government programs or Google searches.

## MODERN EVANGELICALISM AND WILDERNESS THEOLOGY

The point is this: Where and when you write your theology makes all the difference. I suggest the theology of modern evangelicalism, as it peers through the lens of modern experience, is offering the classic *wilderness* perspective shaped by a lack of divine experiences due to sporadic disobedience and distrust.

Our theology is not being shaped by a Promised Land perspective. If we were living in a context of experiencing all that God promises His people, our theology would be markedly different. We would not see suffering as the default condition of God's people. Health would be the general rule and suffering the exception, not a condition to be expected and passively accepted.

We would not feel so dependent in times of decision-making on our own wisdom and intellectual resources. The experience and recognition of the guiding voice of God would be daily bread to our souls.

We would expect to awaken most every day in a state of spiritual and emotional peace, as if we were sitting in gentle breeze under the cool shade of an oak tree, with no one or nothing making us afraid (Micah 4:4).

Instead, we don't anticipate or appropriate a life relatively free of anxieties. And we wiggle our way out of commands such as "Be anxious for nothing" (Philippians 4:6) and "Do not worry" (Matthew 6:25), which imply a Promised Land possibility by joining an unconscious conspiracy of disbelief and labeling a worry-free life as "unrealistic."

How else is this wilderness theology affecting us? I think it causes us to push off into the distant future much of what salvation is intending to provide now. As we saw in Chapter One everyone agrees that there is a "not-yet" to salvation—states of being and doing that God ultimately intends for His people to experience but which have not yet come to pass. But it is the wilderness theology with its lack-induced pessimism robed as realism that unfortunately presumes the not-yet is entirely and unalterably by God's will reserved for future end times.

What if much of the not-yet could be happening now if we made sure our theology was shaped by God's promises, not by our wilderness experience? What *could be* happening now? What *should be* happening now? Those questions will occupy our attention in the rest of this book.

Now let me review what we have covered in the first three chapters, which are designed to get you ready for the never-before-imagined dimensions of salvation.

In *Chapter One* I urged you to stand at the base of the cross and look foward toward what God intended to create through salvation, rather than backward at what God needed to correct.

In *Chapter Two* I urged you to understand and accept the fact that it is necessary to shed old ways of thinking and believing in order to position yourself for what's altogether new.

In this *Chapter Three*, I urged you to base your theology (and all the expectations that flow from it) on God's words not your experiences, and to recognize that our present wilderness theology makes it difficult to imagine the incredible new realities God intends to make possible through salvation.

If these chapters have fulfilled their purpose then you are ready to take a look at three remarkable new possibilities as a result of Jesus' work on the cross that have to do with the kind of beings we can become, the kind of community we can create and the kind of world we can prepare for our coming King.

Now that we have set the stage for looking at three *revelation paradigms*, why not review what we have discussed by considering the questions and sample prayers on the next two pages. After all, that's the functional purpose of this book.

---

### Addendum: An additional word about theological thinking.

I come from a Wesleyan-Arminian theological tradition. Modern students of Wesley's life and theology have coined the phrase "Wesleyan quadrilateral" to capture the four key functional components of the way John Wesley did theology. They say, he used scripture, reason, tradition and experience to come to theological conclusions. I have no argument with that. Most of these scholars also acknowledge as we seek to follow Wesley's model that we, like he, must place scripture in the primary position. Then we let reason, tradition and experience inform our deliberations about understanding, systematizing and applying scripture and scriptural principles. I have no argument with that either.

My word of caution is that we must not only elevate scripture to the primary position in the quadrilateral. We must be very careful to vet what reason, tradition and experience tell us before we use it to vet what we believe scripture is telling us. I fear that in practice the vetting process is only uni-directional. It's as if the content of scripture is what is being examined, questioned, challenged with the other three components being used as witnesses in the examination. But we must be careful to make sure we are examining the witnesses as well. No defense attorney worth his salt would simply let the testimony of a witness against his client stand without questioning the reliability of that witness.

Based on my argument in this chapter, we must always maintain a degree of suspicion about anything reason, tradition and experience have to say about what God's Word means and entails. That is precisely because reason, tradition and experience are always products of one's environment. As much as we may benefit from their input regarding our understanding of scripture, we can just as easily be fooled by their limitations and biases. For example, in his book Salvation Means Creation Healed, historian Howard Snyder provides damning evidence of how reason and tradition truncated the gospel as it pertains to a salvation. Over the centuries a trickle-down theology virtually divorced heaven and earth, created an inaccurate biblical view of the earth and stifled the perpetuation of our proper stewardship role toward the earth. In short, the church couldn't see what scripture clearly said, because reason and tradition did not support it. If you understand the problem of wilderness theology, you'll understand the importance of having a healthy suspicion of reason, tradition and experience.

# REVELATION PARADIGMS - SUMMARY

The purpose of God's saving work through the cross of Jesus Christ was not only to correct what went wrong due to sin but to usher in new realities that would complete His original creation plan. So when we consider what salvation means we should not only stand at the foot of the cross and look back to see the lost glory our Savior wanted to restore, but also look forward to see what new glory our Creator He wants to reveal.

## REFLECTION QUESTIONS

1. Look at where you were 10-20 years ago and where you are today. Describe some "little did you know" events that brought you where you are today.
2. In chapter two we discussed how we need to adjust our priorities about the functional role of righteousness and devotion. Consider these questions:
   - While remaining morally righteous is important, where are you involved in "touching" others with influence that helps them become holy?
   - Maintaining routines of personal devotion are also important, but where could you be more intentional about showing your devotion to Jesus through greater "kingdom" use of your time and talents.
3. What is your general outlook on life? Optimistic? Pessimistic? Realistic? Can you think of any ways in which your outlook is shaped more by your experiences than by God's Word?

## REPENT AND BELIEVE

Lord Jesus, I'll admit I have a tendency to see salvation only as something You did to fix what was broken in me. And I'm glad You did. But I don't tend to think about what You might be doing not just to correct me but to create me in some "great and unsearchable" way. According to Your Word, keeping my incredible future self in mind is what helps me purify myself today (1 John 3:2-3). So I'm taking You at Your Word and calling to You to show me some of what You're planning to do in and through Me so I can participate in Your plan. Amen.

Because God's purpose in salvation was not only to correct what went wrong but to create something new, He wants you to call on Him to show you some "great and unsearchable things." That means you can count on Him to help you get positioned so that you'll be ready for His revelation. You can pray the prayers below for yourself or others and expect a positive response from God. (Always remember to say please and thank you.)

**Prayers for shedding "locked-in" ideas:**
- ✓ Help me learn to ask why I believe something to be true.
- ✓ Help me learn to consider new perspectives without being defensive.

**Prayers for having a "biblically realistic" view of life:**
- ✓ Help me believe Your Word *even if* it does not match my experiences.
- ✓ Help me believe Your Word *even if* it seems unreasonable.
- ✓ Help me believe Your Word *even if* it's contrary to my church's traditions.

**Prayers for faith to expect God to give me revelation:**
- ✓ Give me simple, child-like faith in Your straightforward promises.
- ✓ Let my faith be expressed in direct requests to "show me" Your plans.

**Prayers for living in the "new" ways of righteousness and devotion:**
- ✓ In order to see new things You have in store I need to live in the new ways You've made possible. May my passion for righteousness and devotion be more about effective ministry to others rather than just my being in right relationship with You.

**Prayers for looking forward toward God's future plans:**
- ✓ Open my eyes like never before to everything I read in the Bible that describes what God is wanting to create now because of salvation.

(Add some of your own prayer ideas to this list:)

_____

_____

_____

_____

Now read the Sample Prayer that shows you how to take one of the above bullet points and expand it into a full prayer based on the general idea of revelation paradigms—that the cross of Jesus is about new things God is creating to reveal His glory. After that, prayerfully think about where you might need help from the Lord to be ready to see and receive new insights into the "great and unsearchable things" He is already in the midst of doing.

## A SAMPLE PRAYER

Dear Jesus. So much of the time I do not really invest myself in searching out truth in Your Word on my own and asking for You Youself to show me. Instead I go to church, listen to the pastors and teachers, or sit around in small groups and listen to my friends share their ideas. I know it's important to be taught by leaders and hear the thoughts of fellow Christians. But I'm afraid that has become a substitute for me accepting Your invitation to call on You directly, especially for insight into what You have in store. As a result I'm sure there are things I'm missing or not believing because I'm seeing and hearing only man-made ideas or traditions. Help me prioritize seeking insight and revelation from You directly. Amen.

## JUST ASK ... WRITE YOUR OWN PRAYER

_____

_____

_____

_____

_____

_____

# CHAPTER FOUR

# Creation

People often misunderstand the creative process. Take Thomas Edison for instance. How many times have we heard that Edison failed nearly two thousand times before he finally came upon the carbonized thread filament which made his invention of the affordable light bulb possible? Failed? Those who call 1,999 experimental filaments a failure don't understand the creative process.

Contrary to common belief Thomas Alva Edison did not invent the electric light bulb. By the time he came upon the idea of using thin threads of carbonized Japanese bamboo to create his filament in 1880, more than 20 people had already invented various kinds of incandescent light bulbs dating back to 1802. What no one had created up until that point was a cost-effective and long lasting bulb that could be mass produced and used by the general population to light homes and cities. That involved not only finding the right filament for a single light bulb but developing the entire electric power generation and distribution system that we now take for granted everytime we flip a light switch.

An incandescent bulb no matter how brightly it burns is of no use to the masses unless you can create electricity in large quanitities and deliver it to people's homes. Of the 1,097 patents Edison owned during his life, 356 pertained to the electric light and the public utilities infrastructure. So finding a workable filament was just one small, albeit vital, part of what Edison created: not just a light bulb, but a brand new world of electrical power. By trying 1,999 other filaments he was not failing but searching for a commercially viable component for one aspect of this new electrical world.

Creating a new world is a process. For Edison it involved more than trial and error to find the right filament. It involved creating a grand design and then inventing or organizing a complex array of components into systems—an ecology—that worked together harmoniously.

The creative process is one in which the ultimate goals and products unfold gradually over time... The work of creation is as much about a process as a product.

If we could have entered into Edison's life during this process we would have observed that the creative process is one in which the ultimate goals and products unfold gradually over time. Think sculptor. As he or she chips away at the rock, slowly the finished statue emerges steadily but slowly.

If you had been in Edison's laboratory on the day his carbonized filament had been lit without breaking or burning out for over 1,200 hours, and if you had been there at the moment Edison said something like, "I think we have found our filament," and if you then had broken out into a cheer of delight, "You've done it!" I think Edison would have corrected you very quickly, saying, "No, we have not done anything yet. We have only succeeded in lighting one bulb. The goal is to light the world. We have much work yet ahead."

See? The work of creation is as much about a process as a product. Now follow me as I make a hard right turn...

Imagine if you had been with the Lord God on the sixth and final day of creation, and upon completing the two first human beings you congratulated Him with a resounding, "You've done it!" What would the Lord have said in response? I think He would have said something similar to what I imagined Edison might have said, "No, we are not finished. We have begun a process of creation. We have only succeeded in creating a new earth and two partially complete human beings. The goal is far greater than that, but it will take much more time."

My goal in this chapter is to help you see what the Bible reveals but which most Christians do not appreciate. The work of divine creation was not finished on that primordial sixth day, especially regarding human beings.

This may be a new thought to you and so unfamiliar that it sounds wrong. So bear with me. Suspend your disbelief. Take the tar off the fire and put the feathers down. I hope by the end of the chapter you won't think I'm a heretic.

## PROGRESSIVE CREATION

I think we all can agree that at any given point in time we human beings are not yet everything God intended we should be or will be. We are moving toward true spirituality, but we are not as aware that we are also moving toward some kind of new state of being. John states that explicitly in his first letter:

*Dear friends, now we are children of God, and what we will be has not yet been made known. But we know that when he appears, we shall be like him, for we shall see him as he is.* 1 John 3:2

Paul joins in as he writes with divinely inspired speculation:

*Listen, I tell you a mystery: We will not all sleep, but we will all be changed – in a flash, in the twinkling of an eye, at the last trumpet. For the trumpet will sound, the dead will be raised imperishable, and we will be changed. For the perishable must clothe itself with the imperishable, and the mortal with immortality.*

1 Corinthians 15:51-53

Why would we be changed into something brand new unless it were part of God's plan all along? Clearly the trajectory of our existence is moving upward toward some new glorified state of being that we currently do not experience.

But the beginning of this glorified existence does occur post-mortem. Paul writes elsewhere:

> Now the Lord is the Spirit, and where the Spirit of the Lord is, there is freedom. And we, who with unveiled faces all reflect the Lord's glory, **are being transformed** into his likeness with **ever-increasing glory**, which comes from the Lord, who is the Spirit.
>
> 2 Corinthians 3:17-18

Paul did more than hint at this progressive work of creation when he wrote comments like:

> In all my prayers for all of you, I always pray with joy because of your partnership in the gospel from the first day until now, being confident of this, that **he who began a good work in you will carry it on to completion until the day of Christ Jesus.**
>
> Philippians 1:4-6

We are on a course toward becoming considerably different creatures than when we started out. It is important to note that trajectory is not toward the restoration of something lost and broken. What we once had but lost due to sin—eternal life—and what we once were but weren't anymore—pleasing to God—was restored spiritually the moment Jesus said, "It is finished" from the cross. But clearly, if we read scripture carefully, our lives are moving toward some kind of nature, existence and capacity never before possible.

The question is this: *Did this trajectory begin after our salvation or at the time of creation?*

I will argue that this upward trajectory began at creation, generally for all humankind at the creation of the first man and woman, and specifically for each of us as we were knit together in our mother's womb. I will argue that human beings were not a finished creation when God first breathed breath into their nostrils, nor was he finished creating each of us individually when we emerged breathless from our mother's womb. Had your parents said to God on the day of your birth, "Thank you for what you created and have given us," He would have replied, "I am not done yet."

I will also argue in order for people to become a finished creation God had to create a being He knew would sin. Yes, human sin was an inevitable part of His plan! How could it have been otherwise?

Did God place the man and woman in the garden, give them the command to not eat the fruit and then cross his fingers, mumbling nervously, "I hope, I hope, I hope they do what I commanded"? And then when Eve and Adam succumbed to temptation, did the Lord God say, "Aw shucks! That ruins everything!"?

Certainly not! How could it possibly have been the case that the history of the world hung in the balance of Eve's choice? You mean if Eve had resisted temptation, Jesus never would have had to come and die?

That simply does not square with what scripture teaches. The Salvation Plan is never characterized as Plan B—something God had to jump to only because Eve and Adam took a bite of the forbidden fruit. Instead, what scripture teaches is that God's Plan was formulated before the foundation of the world (1 Peter 1:20). That means God knew beyond a shadow of doubt what Adam and Eve would do. There was never any question about it.

In other words, not just the likelihood but the necessity of sin was built into God's Plan A of creation. There was no Plan B.

## DID GOD WANT PEOPLE TO SIN?

So am I saying that God *wanted* people to sin? This is a question that plagues many of us. I found it recently in a facebook post I happened upon just before I began writing this chapter. It's written by a pastor!

> *Input requested!* [*Note the exclamation mark indicating a tone of frustration and urgency.] *Why would God plant the "Tree of the Knowledge of Good and Evil" in the Garden He placed man in, and give man the freedom of choice? Since God is all-knowing He would have known the consequences. INPUT! Any good insights for a senior high Sunday School class?*

Had your parents said to God on the day of your birth, "Thank you for what you created and have given us," He would have replied, "I am not done yet."

It was necessary for human beings to sin in order for something greater to happen, namely, to become what He wanted them to become.

The responses were very interesting. Many people took a stab at it. The explanations ranged from "God didn't know that would happen" to "That's an interesting question. Good luck!"

Here's my answer. Did God *want* people to sin? Yes and no.

I see this question in the same light as when Jesus let Lazarus die (John 11). Did He *want* Lazarus to die? Did He *want* Martha and Mary to go through the agony of watching their brother die? Of sending word to Jesus but being disappointed that He didn't show up in time? Did Jesus *want* those things to happen? Yes and no.

No, of course he did not relish the thought of what His friends would go through. (Probably that's why He wept at the gravesite. There He was face to face with their pain and sorrow.) But yes, He wanted Lazarus to die so He could demonstrate His power and reveal His glory as the "resurrection and the life" (John 11:25). His delay and Lazarus' death were necessary for something greater to happen and be revealed.

In the same way, no, the Lord God did not want human beings to sin. But yes, it was necessary for them to sin in order for something greater to happen, namely, to become what He wanted them to become. Sin was to become part of the shaping of these new creatures, which explains why God wasn't finished creating them when He filled them with the breath of life. How so?

In order to answer this question I must create a logic pathway for you to follow. Let's begin.

## WHAT MANNER OF MAN?

According to Genesis 1:26 the Lord God's intent for his crowning work of creation was to make a male and female creature, called man, in his image. Consider what it means to be in the image of God. God speaks. God is self-aware. God knows right and wrong. God creates. Some animals can do some of these things in a minimal way.

Whales and dolphins and birds and bees have minimal communication abilities. They make sounds and/or movements that warn, guide, express pleasure or pain, and even "romance" the opposite sex. But they do not have the ability to express abstract thought. Even with all the variations of sounds and squeals and moans a whale can make it will never be able to think and say anything like, "Here I am swimming in the ocean just off the coast of Cape Cod and it's a bright and beautiful day. I think I'll open my mouth for another slurp of 10,000 plankton."

Nor will Magilla gorilla ever be taught to express an opinion about whether his feelings for Priscilla gorilla are true love or just temporary infatuation. In fact, no matter how precocious his linguistic abilities may seem, he will never be able to think, reason, reflect, or meditate on his existence like a human being can. That's because we alone are made in God's image.

Any attempt to close the gap between the most advanced animal and human beings is mere anthropomophic sentimentality. We human beings are in a class with divine likeness all by ourselves.

Every variety of plant and animal may have risen from the primordial soup and evolved to high levels of sophistication. But what makes a human being human could never in a trillion years of chance and advance come from evolution's chain of mutation. Only the Creator's personal touch could have endowed a material being with so many spiritual and moral abilities. Traits of divinity cannot rise from clay. Adam did not spring from reorganized atoms.

So what was the Lord God wanting to create when He created this little god-like being He called man? He was wanting a creature like Him to whom He could relate and who could relate to Him according to the central feature of His nature. He wanted to craft a creature who could love.

Of course, here's the problem. You can't do that with a specially designed string of DNA. Love is a moral trait, not a physical one. Love can only occur if it is chosen.

So what does God have to do first to create that kind of being? He has to endow that creature with free will. That

> What makes a human being human could never in a trillion years of chance and advance come from evolution's chain of mutation.

means God *will not* forcibly control that creature, nor will He allow that creature to be automatically controlled by His natural instincts and impulses, as is the case with other creatures.

Therefore, He must create a creature with moral capacity and conscience, so that he/she can interact with the outside world and other beings from a volitional platform of right and wrong. Then He must make that person relational in nature—just like God Himself—and urge him/her to find their knowledge of right and wrong only through a close relationship with their Creator. Then He must write many of the moral laws on the creatures' consciences and train the creatures to follow the dictates of their conscience. And where their consciences remain uninformed, God must train the creatures to stay attentive to His voice and choose to do what He says.

I believe this is an apt description of what was going at the very beginning of human existence as portrayed in Genesis 2. This new kind of creature was consequently the only creature in all creation that could choose against his/her own desires. That kind of situation is exactly what Genesis 3 is all about: *Would the woman and man choose to follow God's command or their bedazzled desires?*

Of course we know how that moment turned out! Very poorly. Ever since that moment of original sin this freewill-endowed, moral being has been as unpredictably erratic as an excited electron. Thus, God opened the world up to a zillion ways for things to go terribly wrong. And the world has suffered the herky-jerky vacillations of good and evil intent and actions ever since.

Nevertheless, it had to be thus if humankind would ever be able to love in the likeness of God, a claim which I will further support in just a moment.

But wasn't there any other way? Couldn't God have given freewill without things going wrong? You would think so only if you have a shallow view of love.

Yes, God probably could have given freewill and then poured out blessings so abundantly that it would "force"

God's work of creating a being in His image is not something that could have been completed by simply scraping together some clay and breathing life into it.

the human being to be so indebted that no other response but love could have been possible. But would He have in that way created a creature who truly loves Him. Does a seven year old whose grandparents shower her with gifts really love Nana and Papa? When she runs eagerly to greet them every time they come for a visit, is that love in action? It may be some kind of love, but not a very lofty one. There's too much self-interest wrapped up in it. By employing this "lavishing" methodology God would not be creating a being who loves in His image, someone who chooses to love others without the experience or expectation of personal gain.

God's love not only blesses in spite of unwarranted mistreatment, but in anticipation of it.

How do you create that kind of lover? It's probably impossible unless you model it. You must let people watch that kind of love in action and whet their appetite for it.

Are you beginning to see how God's work of creating a being in His image is not something that could have been completed by simply scraping together some clay and breathing life into it? Creating a being who loves like God would take freewill *and* time. But it would take even more than that. It would take two more things for this *imago dei* creature to be complete.

First, God would have to model the true nature and full extent of love. Second, if love is not love unless it is chosen, He would have to create circumstances that would lead human beings to choose that kind of love. Let's explore how the Bible reveals that God did just that.

## WHAT MANNER OF LOVE IS THIS?

If the Bible is a record of anything at all it is the record of the ways God has demonstrated the nature of divine love. This not just one of many divine objectives; it appears that demonstrating love is the Lord God's prime objective. Most importantly, the kind of love He demonstrates confounds human beings. It is beyond their comprehension and capacity. For what sets God's love apart from all other forms of affection is His willingness to bless those who do *not* respect, honor, appreciate, or listen to Him. God's love not only blesses in spite of unwarranted mistreatment, but in anticipation of it.

The late chapters of Deuteronomy record the Lord's words to His people before they entered the Promised Land. Many of those words are affectionate promises of divine presence, provision and protection. In the middle of that *bon voyage* pronouncement He inserts this prophecy about their eventual rebellion when they settle in the Promised Land:

> *And the Lord said to Moses:"You are going to rest with your fathers, and **these people will soon prostitute themselves** to the foreign gods of the land they are entering. **They will forsake me** and **break the covenant** I made with them.*   Deuteronomy 31:16

The amazing thing is God still helped them miraculously cross the Jordan River and take possession of the Promised Land with His gracious presence and victorious power.

Do you see it? God faithfully loves His people and offers His promises knowing in advance that they will reject Him! This is a remarkable demonstration of divine love. But this was not just one isolated incident. The Lord pressed His demonstrations of divine love into their history like a baker kneads yeast into bread dough. So much so that the psalmist would affirm God's unfailing love using the literary rhythm of redundancy by repeating 26 times the Hebrew word for love—*hesed*—in the famous Psalm 136.

> *Give thanks to the Lord, for he is good.*
> *His **love** endures forever.*
> *Give thanks to the God of gods.*
> *His **love** endures forever.*
> *Give thanks to the Lord of lords:*
> *His **love** endures forever.*
>                    Psalm 136:1-3

But His determination to demonstrate the nature of His passion didn't stop even after it was so beautifully expressed in one of the greatest ancient hymns. No, more needed to be shown. So He called one of His prize prophets, Hosea, to outrageously model this unconditional love in his marital life.

*The Lord said to me, "Go, show your love to your wife again, though she is loved by another and is an adulteress. Love her as the Lord loves the Israelites, though they turn to other gods."*   Hosea 3:1

But of course, with a determination to demonstrate love like that coming from the God Who is love, nothing would ultimately suffice until He could come to earth and visibly demonstrate it Himself. That, of course, is what He did in the person of Jesus Christ. He showed how compassion works to the least, to the lost, to the left-out, and even the licentious. He lavished love liberally. But still that was not enough, so He set His eyes on the cross. However, just before that historic day He met with His disciples and did something that left them stupefied. He took off his outer robe, took up a towel and bowl of water, and took on the form of a servant and humbled Himself to wash their feet, even the feet, perhaps especially the feet, of the one who was about to betray Him. And why did He do this? The apostle John explains:

*Jesus knew that the time had come for him to leave this world and go to the Father. Having loved his own who were in the world, he now **showed them the full extent of his love.*** John 13:1

*What manner of love is this?* the disciples wondered. Then He went to the cross. His manner of love had to be lifted up above that upper room where He washed His disciples feet to a high place visible to the world from which He could wash the hearts of every human being.

Demonstrating the nature and manner of divine love—that's been the Lord God's Plan A from before the foundation of the world. And why? Because before the foundation of the world it was His desire to create a being who would love like Him. The only way the world would ever see the nature of His love is if the world could wander from it and still find themselves being invited back into His love. Only that experience could make a freewill-ed creature choose to love like that—like His creator.

Isn't this, after all, exactly what Jesus "demonstrated" in that beautiful moment when He allowed a sexually promiscuous woman to scandalize religious onlookers and wash Jesus' feet, caressing them with her soapy hands and drying them with hair once used occupationally for seduction?

When He was attacked with the blunt question, "How can you allow this woman to do this?" He replied with a moral law as fixed and fundamental as the law of gravity.

> *Therefore, I tell you, her many sins have been forgiven—for she loved much. But he who has been forgiven little loves little.* Luke 7:47

Jesus was not saying He forgave her because of how much she loved Him. Just the opposite. She loved Him so much because of how much He forgave her. That's the law. The more you're forgiven, the more you'll love God.

His crowning work was to create people who would choose to love Him and love like Him. Only if sin entered the world could that ever happen.

So I ask you: Did God want people to sin? In a most sobering and yet wonderful sense, the answer is yes. Because He was engaged in a process of creation. His crowning work was to create people who would choose to love Him and love like Him. Only if sin entered the world could that ever happen. Only over the span of generations of people could that happen.

The cross of Jesus Christ was not about restoring human beings to the pre-sin state they occupied immediately after the sixth day of creation. The creation of whales might have been complete in that primordial "week" of creation, but the creation of human beings couldn't and wouldn't be complete until after the historic transgenerational displays and then the ultimate demonstration of God's love on the cross of Jesus Christ. It was not until then that the love of God was fully revealed.

> *You see, at just the right time, when we were still powerless, Christ died for the ungodly. Very rarely will anyone die for a righteous man, though for a good man someone might possibly dare to die. But **God demonstrates his own love** for us in this: While we were still sinners, Christ died for us.* Romans 5:6-8

The revelation of love requires the reality of sin.

And even still... the work of creating beings in the image of God was not yet complete. Just as a completed light bulb was not the end of Edison's creative work, God still had one more major element to complete this creative process. How to get power to the person?

## WHAT MANNER OF CHOICE IS THIS?

Remember what we said earlier. Love is not love if it is not chosen. That means God must create a way in which people will be changed into beings who love like He does, and become like that *by their choice*.

So He had to make us creatures who could never love like He does unless we were intentionally drawing upon Him for the ability. In other words, He couldn't just transform us into people whose love flowed automatically. The element of choice would still have to be present, every moment of every day. But He made the choice about relationship first, not performance. God is not wanting us merely to choose to love like He loves; He's wanting us to choose Him. "Seek Me. Desire Me, and you will have My love in you."

So here's what God has to do. He allows sin in the world. He allows each of us to succumb to the power of sin. He lets us experience spiritual brokenness and the need of salvation. He demonstrates His love by blessing and saving us in spite of our sin. He waits for us to fall at His feet in love with Him for His love. Such love awakens our moral conscience and resets the bar on what love really is. Our conscience now quickened, unfortunately becomes quickly disquieted and frustrated with our inability to love like God. This, of course, is exactly what God knows will happen. And it's exactly how He planned it. For now, and only now, will this one time lump of clay, cry out from the bottom of his freewill heart, "Please, Lord, I need you to help me love like You!"

And the Creator smiles. "There. That's what I've been working toward and waiting for since before the foundation of the world."

> God is not wanting us merely to choose to love like He loves; He's wanting us to choose Him. "Seek Me. Desire Me, and you will have My love in you."

And He breathes into the creature a second time, this time with His Spirit that not only gives life but now, this time—a time that couldn't have happened any sooner or any other way—He gives love. It's what the apostle Paul called love "shed abroad" in our hearts (Romans 5:5 KJV).

And now God rests.

## WHAT MANNER OF PERSON ARE YOU?

This is what scripture is all about. It is the record of all the ways God showed the nature and extent of His love, to cause people to conceive of an inconceivable love and want to love like that. This is why the apostle Paul made this resounding prayer in Ephesians his personal mission:

> And I pray that you, being rooted and established in love, may have power, together with all the saints, to grasp how wide and long and high and deep is the love of Christ, and to know this love that surpasses knowledge—that you may be filled to the measure of all the fullness of God.    Ephesians 3:17-19

That's how it works. He understood that people have to first come into personal contact with this inconceivable love and experience it for themselves. That's how God creates divine lovers. They have to experience divine love as rebellious people loved back into divine relationship.

Adam and Eve's story is our story. The Bible's history is our history. When we were conceived, God's work of creation began. But it was not finished when we were born. When we were born of water, His work of creation would not be finished until we were born of the Spirit and made perfect in love.

However, that would not happen until we, through our own history of ups and downs and absolute failure and frustration and guilt and shame are confronted with our own absolute inability to love, to measure up to a standard that we admire deep in our hearts but have never achieved in our lives. And we cry out: "Change me! Fill me! Create me! Control me!"

This is the gospel, the good news! It's so much more than getting your sins forgiven. It's the paradigm of *progressive creation*. Everything about the cross, the blood, the sacrifice was to show us the greatest picture of love and, thus, to create in us the deepest desire to come back to God and become like Him.

When we give our lives to God through Jesus the work of creation continues. We aren't actually taken back just to regain something that was lost. Rather, He is moving us forward to something never before gained. Becoming creatures of perfect love.

Ultimately this is the only way in which we will ever be fully "in God's image." It starts by accepting God's love for you in Jesus Christ and then giving your life to His control. When the Spirit controls you, you can love like God loves.

> *Dear friends, let us love one another, for love comes from God. Everyone who loves has been born of God and knows God.* 1 John 4:7

But that doesn't mean you're really good at it. You will continue to need God's help moving you from the inside out.

> *Therefore, my dear friends…continue to work out your salvation with fear and trembling, for it is God who works in you to will and to act according to his good purpose.* Philippians 2:12-13

Everything about the cross, the blood, the sacrifice was to show us the greatest picture of love and, thus, to create in us the deepest desire to come back to God and become like Him.

But still God's creation work isn't finished. His goal is to make you so much like Him, to perfect you in love, that He won't even need to move you any more. It will be you moving you. That means you are going to be gradually changing. You will be involved in a process of putting off your old self, and wanting to

> *…be made new in the attitude of your minds; and to put on the new self, created to be like God.* Ephesians 4:23-24

This process of creation then continues degree by degree, so that…

> *…we, who with unveiled faces all reflect the Lord's glory, are being transformed into his likeness with ever-increasing glory, which comes from the Lord, who is the Spirit.* 2 Corinthians 3:18

It may be hard to detect sometimes, but when you surrender to the control of God's Spirit, progress is guaranteed toward an end goal, so that you can...

*Be confident of this, that he who began a good work in you will carry it on to completion until the day of Christ Jesus.*

Philippians 1:6

And you must become more and more confident in this, because that's also part of the creation process.

*Dear friends, now we are children of God, and what we will be has not yet been made known. But we know that when he appears, we shall be like him, for we shall see him as he is.* **Everyone who has this hope in him purifies himself***, just as he is pure.*   1 John 3:2

God is at work to create you into His likeness, no matter who you are and whether you even believe in Him or not at this point. This is what you were created for: to be like Him—you can. To love like He loves—you will... if you give yourself to the control of His Spirit.

In order to do that for you and all people, God had to allow freewill. That explains so much of the evil in the world. It's not God's fault. Don't blame Him. It had to be that way in order for this amazing plan of creation in His image to occur. The question is whether you will let God finish His work of creation in your life.

~

How does all of this roll into our prayer life? Remember the goal of this *Just Ask* series is to help you gain confidence in your prayers by showing you the heart of God as revealed in His work of salvation. Once you see how God's plan from before the creation of the world was to create human beings—including you—to love just like He loves, don't you think He will answer every prayer you could ever imagine to enable you to do that?

Imagine any possible situation where it is hard for you to love God with all you heart or love your neighbor as yourself. (Is it any wonder now why these are the two greatest commands in light of what God is trying to create?) God created you with a free will, so just ask for His power to love in those situations, and He will do it.

Doc and Liz had spent years building up a sports business with a close friend and partner. They worked hard, but they had grown tired. So when their partner showed interest in buying the business, they prayed about it, said yes and worked out the arrangements for him to pay them the 1.2 million dollars over a few years.

The problem was their friend and former partner never paid them. Anything. They were patient. After all the economy had taken a down turn, and it hit the recreational businesses pretty hard. So they adjusted the agreement to allow him to weather the storm and pay at a slower pace.

He still didn't come through with any money.

*What should we do?* Because they were getting no money from the sale of the business, Doc and Liz could see they would be coming to the end of their resources. They grew more and more angry with him. Bitterness and resentment built up in their hearts, because he was the cause of their struggles.

Friends at church rallied around Doc and Liz when things got worse and they had to start selling their possessions. It was embarrassing to be in that position—a position they were in through no fault of their own. Their former partner was to blame. And the bitterness metastasized.

One day after a church service Doc came to me and asked, "Tell me what you think of this. Am I crazy? I think the Lord is telling me that the only way we will get freed up from this bitterness in our hearts is to tell our former partner that his debt is forgiven. I think I'm supposed to fly out to meet with him, look him in the face and tell him he doesn't owe us anything. See what I mean? You think I'm crazy don't you?"

What did I tell him? Of course I urged them to pray more, count the cost and not do anything suddenly. And if it weren't for my belief in a God who does exactly that kind of thing I would have said, "You're crazy." But I couldn't, because it sounded exactly like something our Love Creator would want one of His progressing creations to do, too. So I said, "Doc, I wouldn't want to advise you to do anything foolish, and I'm not telling you should do it, but I'm just saying what you're talking about is very much like the Lord. So, no, it doesn't sound crazy."

One week later he was on a plane getting ready to descend from the sky and bring his friend and former partner good news of a most radical expression of forgiveness.

And God smiled.

Progressive creation. That's what is going on right now in our lives. Charles Wesley could see it when he penned the words to "Love Divine, All Loves Excelling":

> *Finish, then, thy new creation;*
> *pure and spotless let us be;*
> *let us see thy great salvation*
> *perfectly restored in thee:*
> *changed from glory into glory,*
> *till in heaven we take our place,*
> *till we cast our crowns before thee,*
> *lost in wonder, love and praise.*

Why not move on right now to the application section and interact with the questions and sample prayers.

The **progressive creation** paradigm focuses our attention on the fact that God did not finish creating mankind when he formed Adam and Eve, or formed us in our mother's womb. In order to complete the project of creating us "in His image" He would have to shape us into people who learn the nature of divine love, freely choose it for ourselves and seek Him for receiving it. None of that could occur without the existence of sin and the salvation ministry of the cross.

## REFLECTION QUESTIONS

1. What do you think about this idea that God was not finished creating human beings after the sixth day of creation—that He couldn't have been or they would never have become people who love in His image? Can you think of any other way for that to happen without the entrance of sin and human rebellion in the process?

2. Has there ever been a situation in your life when you knew in advance that someone would hurt you, reject you, turn on you, but you still went ahead and showed them kindness, fulfilled a promise or blessed them in some way? Don't be afraid to share that with the group. It's not bragging. We need to hear these kinds of testimonies. They "spur one another on toward love and good deeds" (Hebrews 10:24).

3. Very often we attempt to love others by "gritting our teeth" and trying hard. But that's not how it works. Divine love is poured into our hearts. Is there any place in your life where you are using the "grit your teeth" method?

## REPENT AND BELIEVE

Dear Lord, I've understood before this that you are not finished with me yet. But up until this point I've always taken that to mean You are still working the sin areas out of my life. I've not fully appreciated that it's more than that: You're still creating me in Your image. My focus is too much on trying not to sin and not enough on wanting to love exactly like You love every moment of every day in every relationship of my life. Help me reorient my expectations. If you would give me the presence of Your Spirit, there is no one under any circumstance I can't love in Your likeness. Praise You. Amen.

Because the **progressive creation paradigm** looks at salvation as the ultimate way God reveals the nature of divine love and shapes us into people who request His ongoing work of creating us in His love-image, you can pray any of the prayers below for yourself or others and expect a positive response from God. (Always remember to say please and thank you.)

**Prayers for God to complete His new creation:**
- ✓ Take my heart and shape it in whatever way You want.
- ✓ Increase my hope and my vision of the loving person I can be with Your help as the One who is continuing to create me.

**Prayers for God to help you see more clearly the full nature of His love:**
- ✓ Make the nature of Your love literally pop off the pages of scripture.
- ✓ Put me back in touch with how much You've blessed me even when I wandered from You.

**Prayers for God to strengthen your free will to choose to love like He loves:**
- ✓ Help me not get so focused on my pains or frustrations that I don't even notice the times and ways I need to be thinking about loving others.
- ✓ Help me to forgive seventy times seven.

**Prayers to be overwhelmed by God's forgiveness:**
- ✓ Help me to see my sin as an affront to You, not just a moral failure.
- ✓ Show me the degree of my sin, so that I will see more fully how much You've forgiven and love You all the more.

**Prayers for the ability to love like God:**
- ✓ Help me to stop gritting my teeth to love others when it is difficult and draw all the more closely to You so that Your love flows through me.

(Add some of your own prayer ideas to this list.)

_____

_____

_____

_____

Note: You can go through each of the prayers above and pray them for others as well as your self.

Now read the Sample Prayer that shows you how to take one of the above bullet points and expand it into a full prayer based on the **progressive creation paradigm**. It's a prayer that is guaranteed God will answer. After that, prayerfully think about where you might need to give the Lord permission to continue His work of finishing His work of creating you in His likeness.

## A SAMPLE PRAYER

Dear Jesus. I have been trying my hardest to love Frank. But he keeps treating me in such condescending ways. It's gotten so I don't even want to be around him, because I just know how he's going to make me feel: like I'm stupid, or can't do anything right. I keep going back to square one, forgiving him in my prayer times and trying to be kind to him. But I know my heart's not in it. I'm just going through the motions because I know that's what I'm supposed to do. Your Word says I'm supposed to love him "from my heart." That's the way You love. So I need You in my heart on this matter. I'm going to stop focusing on trying to love Frank and start focusing on how wonderful Your love is. And let's see what You create in my heart. Amen.

## JUST ASK ... WRITE YOUR OWN PRAYER

_____

_____

_____

_____

_____

_____

# CHAPTER FIVE

# The Miracle Worker

Miracles come in a flash. Young Helen Keller was locked away inside a body that could not see or hear. Her only outlet seemed to be screams and fits of rage against the darkness that rubbed and bumped against her body. She felt a million feelings for which she had no words; never having heard one sound how could she do anything but grunt? Her brilliant mind had a million questions that could not form into a single thought, until...

A patient and loving person came into her life, convinced that there must be a way to reach into the darkness with the light of language.

Annie Sullivan tried everything—like Edison searching for a viable light bulb filament. Then one day the miracle happened. In a flash of miraculous insight somehow Helen Keller grasped the connection between the flow of water over her left hand and the movement of Sullivan's mouth with her right hand saying, "Water!"

Instantly from the moment of discovering just one word, the mind of Helen Keller understood language and the prison doors burst open, ushering her into a world of wisdom and expression she eventually bestowed on a world she could not hear but that would listen to her and her poetry.

Celebrated African-American poet Langston Hughes honored Helen Keller in a poem of the same name:

*She,*
*In the dark,*
*Found light*
*Brighter than many ever see.*
*She,*
*Within herself,*
*Found loveliness,*
*Through the soul's own mastery.*
*And now the world receives*
*From her dower:*
*The message of the strength*
*Of inner power.*

Keller's own poetry testifies to the on-going impact of that first miraculous moment when she learned how to grasp the idea of water and converted it into a life flowing with beauty. Read the first stanza of her 1893 poem *Autumn* and marvel how a person who never saw could pen such colorful lines of visual images:

*Oh, what a glory doth the world put on*
*These peerless, perfect autumn days*
*There is a beautiful spirit of gladness everywhere,*
*The wooded waysides are luminous with brightly painted leaves;*
*The forest-trees with royal grace have donned*
*Their gorgeous autumn tapestries;*
*And even the rocks and fences are broidered*
*With ferns, sumachs and brilliantly tinted ivies.*
*But so exquisitely blended are the lights and shades,*
*The golds, scarlets and purples, that no sense is wearied;*
*For God himself hath painted the landscape.*

Helen Keller's miraculous moment at the water pump is emblematic of a fundamental truth about miracles to which most people are blind. Not only do most miracles happen in a flash, they happen with the most minor causes. We tend to miss this fact: Because miracles have earth-shaking effects, we assume they must have earth-moving causes. Massive adjustments. Multitudinous catalysts. But not so.

Miracles occur mostly by micro-causes. Like atomic energy, one tiny atom splits in half. Like human conception, one tiny sperm impregnates one egg. Like feats of medical healing, one repaired gene or one replaced chemical in the blood or brain reverses dysfunction.

Miracles happen like the Helen Keller moment—something as simple as water on the open palm. The trick to making miracles is doing that one right thing that changes everything—if it exists—at just the right moment. That's what Annie Sullivan did. Something unspectacular produced wonderfully miraculous results.

Let this concept pour over your mind a little while longer. Tiny things, chance encounters, one word, can change the course of whole lives.

About 25 years ago I was doing what I am doing right now: holed up in a motel many hours away from home writing a book. And just like I will do later this afternoon, I went out for an hour of exercise—in those days it was running. (Now my aging knees are grateful it's biking instead.) I was located in a vacation area during the winter off-season, running on a sidewalk past many stores, novelty shops and motels. Coming toward me was another runner. I passed him without any greeting but caught his image out of the corner of my eye. Something about him seemed familiar, so I slowed down with a question in my mind. Apparently something similar happened to him, because we both stopped and turned around at the same time about 30 feet apart. "Andy?" I said.

"Doug?"

He was a college friend I hadn't had any contact with for 17 years! For the next 20 minutes we were caught up in dumbfounded conversation about this chance encounter.

> Miracles occur mostly by micro-causes. Tiny things, chance encounters, one word, can change the course of whole lives.

As we talked he found out I was the president of a small struggling Christian boarding school in Appalachia, and I found out he had become very wealthy in several business ventures in the midwest. We exchanged contact information still surprised by this unlikely meeting, and went on our way.

That "chance" encounter turned out to be a miracle of divine provision for the school, as this friend became a major donor for desperately needed building projects and improvements that have since helped the school thrive with international impact.

Miracles are often matters of major good resulting from minor events. What makes them miracles is that God is behind those tweaks and twists that lead to major turns. You'll never convince me that my encounter with Andy was anything other than something God triggered with the flick of His little finger. "All I need to do is have Doug and Andy bump into each other." Flick!

I could spend the rest of my time in this book telling other stories like this one to illustrate how much of my life—and probably yours too—has been miracle-propelled in just this way.

One little event, a chance encounter, an aptly spoken word, a fleeting thought which in retrospect were nothing less than divinely triggered. However, that point being made, it's time to move on and talk about God—the ultimate miracle worker—and another paradigm of salvation: *the good works paradigm.*

In the last chapter we examined the progressive creation paradigm in which we saw that God's plan of creation required a plan for sin and salvation that would produce human beings who would choose to love like God. God's work of creating human beings in clay is not complete until we are created in Christ. That's another way to look forward from the cross to see what God has in store. Paul adopted this forward-looking perspective when he wrote:

> *For we are God's workmanship, **created in Christ Jesus to do good works**, which God prepared in advance for us to do.*
>
> Ephesians 2:10

> Miracles are often matters of major good resulting from minor events. What makes them miracles is that God is behind those tweaks and twists that lead to major turns.

From this perspective it is easy to see that we must look at salvation from the perspective of good works—not good works in order to be saved, but good works because we are saved. This dovetails nicely with the progressive creation paradigm in which we saw God's passion to draw us into a chosen life of divine love. For love always manifests itself in good works. Love wants nothing less than the highest and best possible blessings to come to all people.

It is ridiculous to think that you can be loving your neighbors as yourself and not asking how you can be part of bringing blessing into their lives. This is what God wants. You are His workmanship from creation in clay to creation in Christ to do good works—works of divine love, works that He prepared in advance for you to do.

But here's the thing. We have to set our sights higher than we often do on the nature of these good works. We read verses about feeding the hungry, clothing the naked, and think of those good works as the ultimate standard of love. And they are, to be sure, inherently beautiful and pleasing to God. Perhaps even lofty enough to be consider the *penultimate* good works, but they are not the *ultimate*. The ultimate good works of God are miracles—that is, works that only God can do. This is the standard of true good works for which we were created in Christ.

We were created to be miracle workers. Our salvation is not complete unless and until we choose this path of expressing God's love in His likeness. There is no doubt His likeness necessarily involves miracles of grace and assistance. So let's spend time looking more closely at the *good works* salvation makes possible and how we can pursue accomplishing them.

## JESUS, OUR MODEL MIRACLE WORKER

To do so, we simply look again at Jesus. He is the visible embodiment of divine love in action. When He walked the Galilean paths His good works were

> Our salvation is not complete unless and until we choose this path of expressing God's love in His likeness. There is no doubt His likeness necessarily involves miracles of grace and assistance.

most often miraculous in nature. Certainly He loved people in common ways: kind words, tender touches, personal presence, thoughtful counsel. But there is no way to overstate His record of showing love through doing for people what only God could do; that is to say, He worked miracles for people.

In the gospels there are five occasions in which Jesus is specifically said to have been acting with "compassion." It is not that He wasn't acting with compassion on many or even all other occasions, but there must have been something about these moments that jumped off the page at the onlooking disciples as examples of good works done with unique compassion. Four of the five are clearly associated with supernatural miracles. Let's review them:

### Healing the multitudes:

*Jesus went through all the towns and villages, teaching in their synagogues, preaching the good news of the kingdom and healing every disease and sickness. When he saw the crowds, **he had compassion on them**, because they were harassed and helpless, like sheep without a shepherd.* Matthew 9:35-36

*When Jesus heard what had happened, he withdrew by boat privately to a solitary place. Hearing of this, the crowds followed him on foot from the towns. When Jesus landed and saw a large crowd, he had compassion on them and healed their sick.*

Matthew 14:13-14

### Multiplication of bread for the multitude:

*Jesus called his disciples to him and said, "**I have compassion for these people**; they have already been with me three days and have nothing to eat. I do not want to send them away hungry, or they may collapse on the way."*

*His disciples answered, "Where could we get enough bread in this remote place to feed such a crowd?"*

*"How many loaves do you have?" Jesus asked.*

*"Seven," they replied, "and a few small fish."*

*He told the crowd to sit down on the ground. Then he took the seven loaves and the fish, and when he had given thanks, he broke them and gave them to the disciples, and they in turn to the people. They all ate and were satisfied. Afterward the disciples picked up seven basketfuls of broken pieces that were left over. The number of those who ate was four thousand, besides women and children.*

Matthew 15:32-38

**Healing of two blind men:**

*Two blind men were sitting by the roadside, and when they heard that Jesus was going by, they shouted, "Lord, Son of David, have mercy on us!"*

*The crowd rebuked them and told them to be quiet, but they shouted all the louder, "Lord, Son of David, have mercy on us!"*

*Jesus stopped and called them. "What do you want me to do for you?" he asked.*

*"Lord," they answered, "we want our sight."*

**Jesus had compassion on them** *and touched their eyes. Immediately they received their sight and followed him.*

Matthew 20:30-34

**Healing of a man with a leprous hand:**

*A man with leprosy came to him and begged him on his knees, "If you are willing, you can make me clean."*

**Filled with compassion**, *Jesus reached out his hand and touched the man. "I am willing," he said. "Be clean!" Immediately the leprosy left him and he was cured.*   Mark 1:40-42

Clearly this benchmark compassion of Jesus longs to be expressed in working miracles, apparently in more than exceptional cases. His good works were good precisely because they provided the miraculous solution to menacing problems. As long as there are people who need God's love, they will need a miracle worker.

But should those miracle workers be ordinary people like you and me? Should we presume to pursue those good works?

## GOOD, BETTER, BEST: THE ETHICS OF LOVE

Whenever people use the word "should" in formal or informal communication they are making an ethical statement. So when I argue, as I am, that God's plan of salvation is the continuation of His original plan to create human beings in His image, and that His image seen in the person of Jesus Christ reveals a kind of love that works miracles, and that all Christians *should* intend to be miracle workers as well, I am making an ethical statement. Seeking to be a miracle worker is a right thing to do. Neglecting that role is wrong.

But isn't that going a little too far? Is a person really being unethical if he/she doesn't pursue acts of miracle working? As gently and humbly as possible I must say yes. Let me explain.

You've probably seen stores that sell products ranked in three categories: good, better and best. Do you want to buy a paint brush? You can buy the good one for $4.99, the better one for $6.99 or the best one for $8.99. Your decision will be based on whether the job you have to do requires the best brush they have to offer. Or can you do the job well enough with either of the two lesser quality brushes? That's your decision and it's not an ethical one, unless of course you're painting someone else's house and choosing a lesser quality brush will result in a poorer quality paint job.

> Seeking to be a miracle worker is a right thing to do. Neglecting that role is wrong.

In the same way ethical matters can be analyzed according to the "good-better-best" grid. However, here's the rub. Traditionally it has been an accepted ethical standard that simply choosing to do something good is not automatically good. How can that be? Isn't doing a good thing always a good thing? No.

When could it ever be the case that doing a good thing is not good? Answer: *when you had it within your power to do something better.*

For example, giving a person a blessing and a kind word is a good thing. But according to Jesus' brother James, giving a blessing is not a good thing, if you could have done something more. In that case you *should* have done more.

> *Suppose a brother or sister is without clothes and daily food. If one of you says to him, "Go, I wish you well; keep warm and well fed," but does nothing about his physical needs, what good is it?*
>
> James 2:15-16

The apostle John echoes that same ethical standard and goes so far as saying that the love of God is not in him.

> *If anyone has material possessions and sees his brother in need but has no pity on him, how can the love of God be in him? Dear children, let us not love with words or tongue but with actions and in truth.*   1 John 3:16-18

Kind words of concern are good, but doing something practical to meet a person's needs is better. To not have chosen the "better" is unethical. But here's the greater rub. Both of those verses compare the *good* with the *better*. Let's format a verse that sounds similar to James 2:15-16, but this time rather than comparing something good with something better, let's compare the *better* with the *best*.

> *Suppose a brother or sister is struggling with a severe physical malady. If one of you says to him, "Here's money to help you with your medical expenses, and I'll help the church organize a plan to bring food in,"* [better] *but does nothing to remedy the physical malady if possible* [best], *what good is it?*

Of course, that's not an actual Bible verse. However, it fits the same pattern and harmonizes with the same ethical standard stated in James. And I would add that it is also fitting to paraphrase similarly the question John asked in 1 John 2:15-16.

> *If anyone has powerful spiritual resources* [best] *and sees his brother in need but only addresses His problem with material resources* [better], *how can the love of God be in him?*

But that is the $64,000 question. Does the average Christian have these powerful spiritual resources to give? Can we (*should we*) go so far as to say the famous words of the apostle Peter to people around us?

> *"Silver or gold I do not have, but what I have I give you. In the name of Jesus Christ of Nazareth, walk."* Acts 3:6

Do we in fact have the potential, as we stand before the display of God's love, to access the *best* that love can give? Or are we limited in most cases to selecting only the *good* or the *better* works?

You may disagree that the *best* way, namely miracle working ability, is available to us. But based on the principles of ethics, all of us must at least be willing to ask, "What is the best possible way I am permitted to express love in this case?" and not settle for something less.

As I read about Jesus and watch how His compassion for people showed itself, and as I see in Him the heart of God, and as I take seriously God's original plan to create people who love in His image, I simply cannot imagine any other scenario. Miracle working ability must be part of His design for all of His people, not just some uniquely endowed "Special Forces" unit.

In fact, it was exactly when Jesus saw the masses and their helplessness and was involved in healing all who came to Him that He commanded His disciples to pray that the Lord would send out *workers* into the harvest.

> *Jesus went through all the towns and villages, teaching in their synagogues, preaching the good news of the kingdom and **healing every disease and sickness**. When he saw the crowds, **he had compassion on them**, because they were harassed and helpless, like sheep without a shepherd. Then he said to his disciples, "The harvest is plentiful but the workers are few. Ask the Lord of the harvest, therefore, to **send out workers** into his harvest field.*
>
> Matthew 9:35-38

The Greek word that captured what He meant in Aramaic by the word "workers" is the word *ergates* (whose root word *ergon*) is a broadly connoted word. But very importantly in the Judeo-Christian biblical context *ergon* carries moral as well as miraculous connotations. It is in fact the word used of the Lord God in the Genesis 2 (Greek Septuagint) creation account. It is also the word most commonly used, especially by John, in the New Testament for the divine works of God.

Consequently, when Jesus commands His disciples to ask the Lord of the harvest to "send out workers" it makes interpretive sense to understand this to mean a request not just for unskilled laborers, but craftsman who are skilled and creative in performing divine works.

Plus, we should not miss the overtones of commissioning in the verb "send out." Does it not echo the moment of Jesus sending out His disciples to "heal the sick, raise the dead, cleanse those who have leprosy, drive out demons" (Matthew 10:8)? And this, by the way, is what He did immediately following the plea for more workers. He, the Lord of the harvest, sent out people to do miraculous works.

It seems quite clear that we, the people of God, have before us the potential to be *compassion-impelled miracle workers* in the image of our Lord. Therefore, the ethics of love also compels us never to settle for less than the best we can do in His name.

In the previous chapter on progressive creation we discovered that creation is not complete until we become people who love in the likeness of God. At the end of that chapter we focused on the nature of His love, which is to love those who don't love you. Now we must extend our grasp of progressive creation and recognize that we are also to become like our Lord in terms of working miracles. God's plan of creation/salvation is that we become people who do good works. According to basic ethics, good works are only good if they provide the best that is possible. We must pursue miraculous works.

Since that is God's goal, I want to show you two directions to focus your attention in order to be a miracle worker.

> We, the people of God, have before us the potential to be compassion-impelled miracle workers in the image of our Lord.

## THE MECHANICS OF WORKING MIRACLES

From this point we could easily write a whole book about faith, since faith is required to work miracles. That needs no support. But sometimes in our haste to talk about faith, which is the triggering cause of miracles, we fail to understand the mechanics of miracles and don't know where to focus our faith. So let's go back to where this chapter started: Helen Keller's miraculous moment.

As we acknowledged, most major changes occur due to some very small catalyst. A miracle is a major change, but in many cases it only takes one small act. Many of the Biblical miracles exemplify that principle:

- *The woman healed of her twelve-year bleeding problem* focused on one small act: touching the hem of Jesus' garment. Up until that point she was trying to move heaven and earth to fix her problem, spending all her money on every doctor she could find. That major effort was a dead end. But the tip of her fingers touching a linen hem? Immediately, a miracle of healing occurred.

- *Zaccheus' whole life was trapped in greed and held in public scorn.* Even though he had become financially wealthy, he was spiritually and socially poor. We don't know whether he was wanting a complete life transformation or just a better view of Jesus, but a miracle of transformation occurred. The key to life change was not a matter of entering a self-help course or following a rigorous path of spiritual disciplines. The miracle of transformation was set in motion the moment he did one little act of climbing a tree.

- *More than ten thousand people were hungry and needed a refreshing meal.* They weren't starving, but grace and kindness called for someone to try to help them eat. Jesus' disciples assumed the only solution was to send the crowd away to fend for themselves in the nearest town. But when Jesus challenged the disciples to do something about it personally, they could only conceive of addressing the situation with an outlay of big bucks they didn't have. Little did they know all it took was what little they had—five loaves of bread and two fish. It was laughably meager in light of the multitude. But that's all the miracle required.

That is often the mechanics of a miracle. One right thing at just the right time and—voila!—everything changes. Touching a hem. Climbing a tree. Giving up supper.

If that's the case then our primary focus as miracle workers must be on doing or saying this "one right thing at just the right time." How do we find out what that is? By seeking the wisdom of the Lord. In other words, when wanting to work a miracle out of compassion for others, don't try doing a "big thing." Instead draw close to the Lord and ask Him to give you that "one thing" you can pray, do or say. That's what wisdom is. It's knowing the right thing to do and when to do it.

Lots of people don't make this causal connection between wisdom and miracles. But it's stated plainly at the beginning of Jesus' ministry. In the early chapter of Mark's gospel we read about many wonderful miracles Jesus performed, seemingly one after another. It left many people astounded, but also confused. They couldn't imagine a lowly carpenter from Nazareth could do and say things like Jesus. In fact, many people were voicing downright insulting things about His background and upbringing. But in the course of their derogatory comments, they had to admit His abilities were a puzzle. It's in one particular comment that we see this connection they made between wisdom and miracles:

> When the Sabbath came, he began to teach in the synagogue, and many who heard him were amazed. "Where did this man get these things?" they asked. "What's this **wisdom** that has been given him, that he even does **miracles**?"
>
> Mark 6:2

We don't appreciate wisdom in the way Jewish people did. They saw it as the way God accomplished His divine work—by His wisdom.

> God made the earth by his power; he founded the world by his wisdom and stretched out the heavens by his understanding.
>
> Jeremiah 10:12

The parallelism of Hebrew poetry allows us to draw a tight cord around wisdom and causation in how God accomplishes His work. Consequently, here's the secret to becoming a miracle worker: *You are in the best position to see God's divine power expressed in and through your life if you seek first and foremost, not miracles but, His wisdom.* It is then that you will find yourself discovering the one right thing to pray, do or say at just the right time that results in a miracle in someone's life.

This is what God created you for. This is what He saved you for. This is the *best* way to express divine love. **Don't try** to do miracles; **you will do** miracles if you seek God's wisdom.

~

Here's how it works. I had a friend Peter who was trapped in a season of serious depression. Depression is a gray area not only emotionally but diagnostically. When is it clinical? When is it chemical? When is it genetic? When is it a result of poor life choices, or stress? When is it demonic or sin-induced? There is nothing wrong with trying to find out the answer to this question. But our common mistake is to think we must answer the question before we take any steps to address it. This is understandable. We don't want to tell a person to try making some "better choices" if it is a problem with brain chemistry, rather than sleep habits.

So after several agonizing weeks of watching Peter sink lower and lower, I was at a loss about what to do to help. I tried to encourage him, to lift him up with words, to avoid saying anything that would make him feel guilty. But nothing was helping. As he sank deeper into his psychic sadness, he seemed to drift farther away in the fog.

Seek God's wisdom. You will find yourself discovering the one right thing to pray, do or say at just the right time that results in a miracle in someone's life.

In my desperation I finally became more determined to seek the Lord for guidance. Of course I should have done that sooner, but God graciously never said, "You should have done this sooner. Now you're going to have to just wait a little while."

Instead, within a brief period of time—maybe a half hour of prayer, pleading really—I suddenly knew what I was supposed to do and say. I *knew* because God's voice often speaks thoughts that are either opposite or perpendicular to my normal way of thinking or current stream of thought. Which is to say, an idea comes out of the blue. I think something I've never heard or thought before. And I don't labor to form it in my mind like I do when I am trying to come up with what to write on a birthday card. It's just there in one instant package.

Sensing God's guidance may work differently for you, but the Bible promises that when we consistently draw close to the Lord we come to recognize His voice. And that "perpendicular-to-stream-of-consciousness", "complete-all-at-once" package is how God's voice *sounds* to my spiritual ears.

Here's what I heard, I believe, from the Lord on that occasion: "Doug, you've been trying to make Peter feel better and get over this depression by reminding him that God loves him. That's not what he needs to hear. Don't say, "God loves you." Tell him, "You love God.""

Instantly I knew that was the perfect thing. I never would have thought of it, but when the idea of reversing the common words of encouragement came to my mind, it all made sense, and I saw the heart of Peter's struggle. For a variety or reasons he had been living his life in the shadows of guilt and self-doubt. *I know I'm supposed to love God with my whole heart, but I don't think I do. God must be very disappointed in what a poor disciple I am.*

Instantly I popped to my feet and was like a football player in the locker room nearly bursting to get out on the field for the big game. It was a Wednesday night about an hour before the mid-week prayer meeting. So I called Peter and asked him to meet me in my office about fifteen minutes before church started.

"I've got something to tell you." I could sense he was suspicious and a little scared of what I would say, so I reassured him, "Don't worry it's nothing bad. I just want to tell you face to face."

He showed up just as I asked. His countenance was the visual definition of what the Bible calls "downcast." He couldn't lift his head to look me in the eye. I walked over to him—to this day I can see exactly where we both were standing beside my desk—and simply said, "Peter, I believe the Lord wants me to say just one thing to you...Here it is: You love God."

Then something amazing happened. It was like a wall of breath hit him and he stumbled backwards, gasped and began to cry. It was an experience I have since seen on a few other occasions. The right words—meaning of course words from the Lord—spoken at just the right time can produce this kind of reaction.

And Peter's depression was lifted.* It was a miracle. But all it took was speaking three words and flip-flopping the normal order of the first and third word.

Events like that have happened enough in my life—I mean dozens and dozens of times—that I am sure the words of Isaiah 50:4 describe both what God wants for us and what is to be the norm for miracle workers looking for His transforming, miracle working wisdom:

*The Sovereign Lord has given me an instructed tongue,*
*to know the word that sustains the weary.*
*He wakens me morning by morning,*
*wakens my ear to listen like one being taught.*

The mechanics of miracle working involves often the littlest thing that will move mountains. Seed-sized faith. A hand under a water pump. The Lord's plan is to create you in His image. Jesus worked miracles, but according to Him they were always the result of Him simply hearing and doing only what the Father told Him. He didn't go around trying to do miracles; He only tried to listen to find the Father's wisdom: the one right thing done at just the right time. After singling out a lame man who had never walked for healing, He explained:

*"I tell you the truth, the Son can do nothing by himself; he can do only what he sees his Father doing."* John 5:19

---

*In the interest of full disclosure I must tell you that years later he sank again into depression, but that was due to persistent disobedient choices. Miracles in a person's life do not guarantee their perseverance or future devotion. This does not negate the reality of the instantaneous transformative miracle that took place. Even Jesus recognized the possibility of relapse and in one famous case urged a healed lame man not to fall back into sin (John 5:14).

The things Jesus taught and the way He taught left people amazed. His memorable statements and brief parables changed not only their world, but the world's history. He spoke relatively few words in comparison to the libraries of books people have written. They were miracle-working words. But they weren't His words. By His own admission they all came from the Father (John 12:49).

Again, the point is this: God's plan of creation is to make us in His image. He is doing this in your life and mine even now because of what the cross of salvation made possible: being created *in Christ* to do good works. *Good:* meaning the best that can be done. The *best:* often meaning miraculous works. But miracles often happen through little things—one right thing at just the right time—discovered in a close listening relationship with our heavenly Father.

This should give you great confidence in prayer. If it is God's plan from before the creation of the world to make people in His image, then He will answer your prayers for His wisdom when you are ready to do the good, sometimes miraculous, works He has created you to do.

## THE PANORAMA OF MIRACLE WORKING

There is a second element in the mechanics of miracle working. It may seem like I'm speaking out of both sides of my mouth after I have spent so much time emphasizing the importance of keeping your focus on the small element of "one right thing at just the right time." But now I must tell you to step back and think big.

Yes, the trigger for a miracle is often one small thing at the right time. However, most often the possibility of a miracle involves not being thrown off by a problem or situation seeming "too big" to handle. Feeding 5000 hungry people? The disciples were tempted to pass off the idea as ridiculous. Ultimately one small thing—five loaves and two fish—did the trick, but that never would have happened had the disciples rejected the possibility of a miracle altogether.

Too often that's what we do. Situations requiring a miracle seem too big and daunting, so we don't even attempt a miraculous work. It's a simple point, but it is crucial. People of prayer, especially, must train ourselves never to see any situation as beyond God's miracle working power. We may not know for sure what God wants to do. But if we rule out any possibility before we acknowledge that nothing is too big for God, we won't even seek His wonderful wisdom that may give us the "one right thing at just the right time" to pray, do or say.

In fact, I am going so far as to say that you should lean headlong into impossible situations. Don't run from big challenges. There are needs in your world—local, regional and global—waiting for a "miracle worker" to come along and say, "This is just the kind of thing God loves to fix."

Ask the big questions. It's fine to go ahead and help at the local food pantry. But don't stop there. Think bigger: *What can we do to arrest poverty in our community?*

It's fine to keep praying for people who are struggling with physical problems. But think bigger: *What can we do to raise the level of health so that we are preventing the many physical problems that are diet and lifestyle related?*

The Lord has a panoramic view of human need. Yes, he cares for individuals, but His passion is to serve multitudes, to change communities, to redeem whole cultures. We must shift our hearts in that direction. Nothing opens the door for a miracle wider than a big challenge. Don't shy away. Often that's the best way to express love.

Remember our discussion of ethics? We said if you choose to do a good thing but have within your power to do something better, you have made a wrong choice. Let's apply that to this issue of taking on big challenges.

Think about the parable of the Good Samaritan. Remember how an innocent traveler was beaten, robbed and left for dead alongside the road? Both a priest and a Levite avoided him due to fear and the excuse of "pressing business" in Jerusalem. But the good Samaritan did not.

> *But a Samaritan, as he traveled, came where the man was; and when he saw him, he took pity on him. He went to him and bandaged his wounds, pouring on oil and wine. Then he put the man on his own donkey, took him to an inn and took care of him. The next day he took out two silver coins and gave them to the innkeeper. "Look after him," he said, "and when I return, I will reimburse you for any extra expense you may have."* Luke 10:33-35

The Samaritan is commended for his go-the-extra-mile compassion. And rightly so. He did what was *good.* But now let's amend the story slightly.

Imagine the Samaritan getting on his way after having cared for the victim and a half hour later comes across another robbery victim. Once again, godly compassion compels him to rescue the wounded traveler, and he repeats his care-giving actions. That's even *better!*

But what if it happens again and again and again? Shouldn't it dawn on him at some point that the problem that needs to be fixed is not the wounded people, but their susceptibility to attack on the dark road. He should probably think: *If I really care about people, I wouldn't want them to be hurt in the first place! What can I do? We need a bigger solution than what I can provide by scooping these people up and putting them on my donkey.*

If this parable were set in modern times, we would immediately see that love in action should be directed more toward prevention than rescue. Prevention is *best.* That's the big problem that requires a miraculous work. "This road needs a miracle of streetlights!"

I can see heaven full of miracles waiting to be born on earth if only God's people were willing to see human needs and address the systemic problems that seem way too big for any one person.

In summary, in His work of salvation and progressive creation God wants to shape people who love like He loves. That means we must become, like Him, a miracle worker. That will happen in two ways: seek Him for the small words and deeds that trigger miracles, and don't shy away from big problems that leave the multitude harassed and helpless.

As always, take some time now to process what you have read by practicing prayers that are born out of this *miracle worker paradigm.*

> Nothing opens the door for a miracle wider than a big challenge. Don't shy away. Often that's the best way to express love.

## PARADIGM IN BRIEF

The **miracle worker paradigm** is a functional extension of the progressive creation paradigm in that it focuses our attention on the fact that God saves us to create us "in Christ" to do good works and love like He does—in the best ways possible— often requiring that we engage in miraculous works.

## REFLECTION QUESTIONS

1. Can you think of a major change in your life that occurred as a result of just one small event, word or adjustment?

2. In this chapter we called attention to a few examples in scripture where Jesus or the disciples did "one right thing at just the right time" and something miraculous occurred. But there are many others. Try to name two or three more. Here's one for starters: Israel kept winning it's battle as long as Aaron and Hur helped support Moses' upraised arms (Exodus 17:12).

3. On a scale of "good, better, and best" where does your church tend to focus the efforts of your congregation? What would it take to help move it toward a passion for the "best" possible acts of ministry and love?

4. If we all are supposed to be "miracle workers" what difference does it make to know that we should seek the Lord and not miracles?

5. Look around. Are there some "huge challenges" that you and your church could take on that would take a miracle to pull off?

## REPENT AND BELIEVE

Lord Jesus, this has been a very convicting chapter. Plus it has stretched my thinking. I have not been inclined to think of myself as a miracle worker. Nor have I been in the habit of seeking the possibility of engaging in miraculous works in the course of fulfilling Your command to "love my neighbor as myself." But now come to think of it, if I hope the Lord would work miraculously for me, then I guess I should want to do so for others. So I confess that I have been settling for "good" works but not the "best" works that might be possible. Help me reorient my faith and practice to join Your miraculous works when You show me how. Amen.

Because God's purpose in salvation was not just to correct what went wrong but to create new things, He wants to create you in Christ Jesus to love like He loves and perform the "good works" for which you were created in the first place. So you can pray any of the requests below for yourself or others and expect a positive response from God. (Always remember to say please and thank you.)

**Prayers for owning my ethical responsibility to do miraculous works:**
- ✓ Help me be honest with myself and You Lord.
- ✓ Help me develop a habit of ranking my options according to the "good, better, best" grid.
- ✓ Help me always pursue the "best" expression of love and not settle for anything less without becoming "neurotic." (see addendum on page 101)

**Prayers for faith to fulfill my role as a miracle worker:**
- ✓ Let the words of scripture build my faith to be a miracle worker.
- ✓ Every time I step out in this role please confirm my obedience.

**Prayers for eyes to see opportunities for doing miraculous work:**
- ✓ Change my default reaction to look for human rather than divine solutions.
- ✓ Increase my hunger for the display of Your glory through miracles.

**Prayers for divine wisdom for miraculous work:**
- ✓ Give me an expectation that You will show me what to do or say.
- ✓ Help me never to run ahead on my own until I am sure You have spoken.

**Prayers for taking on huge challenges:**
- ✓ Help me see the systemic causes of individual problems.
- ✓ Help me give my meager resources and believe they can be multiplied when placed in Your hands and used with faith and divine wisdom.

(Add some of your own prayer ideas to this list:)

_____

_____

_____

_____

Now read the Sample Prayer that shows you how to take one of the above bullet points and expand it into a full prayer based on the miracle worker paradigm— that the ethics of love requires that we offer the best possible expression of compassion. After that, prayerfully think about where you might need help from the Lord to do the works He created you to do—including miraculous ones.

## A SAMPLE PRAYER

Dear Jesus. I get in conversations with people all the time who are facing problems. Most of them are ordinary problems, but some are quite severe. Probably because they are mostly common, I get into the habit of only thinking about ordinary solutions: take some pills, get rid of some stress, change your job, go see a counselor, look it up on the internet, get into an accountability group... or whatever. None of this is bad advice. It's just that You may want to do something better, something more, but I never even go there in my head. I'm asking You to totally change my orientation so that the first thing I think about is that You may want to work a miracle through me in this situation before I just pass on the common solutions. Amen.

## JUST ASK ... WRITE YOUR OWN PRAYER

_____

_____

_____

_____

_____

_____

**\*ADDENDUM: How to Pursue the "Best" and Not to Become Neutoric.**

I have knwon many Christians who always seem to be living under a cloud of fear that they are never doing enough or being good enough. For some people that's just a weakness of their personality. Their egos lack confidence, and they always worry about whether they are pleasing other people. For others the problem is a failure to understand and receive the full measure of God's available grace. They think that the littlest wrong move ruins everything.

Whatever the case my be, it also seems that this problem increases in many Christians as they grow older, especially as they come closer to the end of life. "What if I haven't done enough, and haven't been pleasing to the Master?"

If you have any tendency in this direction, please listen carefully. I know that the "good, better, best" grid plays right into the potential for great worry. The minute I tell you that doing something good if you could have done something better is a wrong choice, you start getting worried about everything. Does that mean I shouldn't lift up that ethical standard? Does that mean you should avoid trying to live up to that standard? That's the advice some counselors give to people who struggle with guilt and worries of this sort. But is that the way to handle the problem? Avoid the guilt by lowering the standard? Of course not.

Instead, we must recognize that the Lord has given one wonderful way out of these kinds of fears. Stay close to Him. Learn to recognize His voice. Never listen to general feelings of guilt. Listen only to specific conviction. When you are actually in the wrong, the Holy Spirit addresses it point blank. He doesn't leave you wondering, living under a cloud of unspecified shame.

Now, as it pertains to this matter of "miracle working." You may find yourself worrying from situation to situation, "Is this a miracle working time? Is this a miracle working time? I want to do what's best! Should I be offering to pray for someone's healing, rather than encouraging them to go to the doctor?" If you find that happening, remember the same principle applies to miracle working as to dealing with guilt. Stay close to the Lord. Yes, you are under general orders to do what's best to love others and that may occasionally involve miracle working. But you are not under general orders to do miracles. If you are to step out in an act of miracle working, the Lord will get very specific. You will have a strong impulse to do so. If that isn't there, don't worry. As long as you are guarding your relationship with the Lord and not wandering from Him in your life, you will pick up those signals when He sends them. Otherwise, if you're not getting specific instructions, you're off the hook. Relax. Even Jesus said he only did what the Father told Him to do. So one day he was actually at a healing pool with scores of sick people around, but he worked only one miracle... because that's all He heard from His Father.

# CHAPTER SIX

# Utopia

Since the early 1960s there are people who have been listening carefully. Methodically. Sacrificially. Although often ridiculed for wasting their time and money on pointless pursuits, they remain vigilant. They are convinced that there must be extraterrestrial intelligence in our galaxy. And they are listening for interstellar communications.

Physicists Giuseppe Cocconi and Philip Morrison sparked this modern exploration with their article "Searching for Interstellar Communications" in a 1959 issue of *Nature* magazine.

It was not a big-bang moment in the universe of astrophysics, but it did have enough impact to stimulate astronomer Frank Drake to work out an equation to predict the number of possible solar systems in the Milky Way galaxy that could produce intelligent life advanced enough to be sending communications into space. His so-called "Drake Equation" is demonstrably inaccurate, because several of its seven factors can be only matters of speculation. In spite of its apparent inaccuracy, many people argue that the number of planets that could have produced advanced intelligent civilizations is in the millions. This possibility was so compelling that it attracted ten high-power thinkers—including the famous Carl Sagan—to meet together at the first SETI (Search for Extraterrestrial Intelligence) gathering in 1961.

By now it's been over a half century of listening. Nothing yet. Not a peep.

People wonder why. If there are so many planets that could produce life, that could evolve with intelligence, that could have advanced to the point where they had become, as astronomer Aleksandr Zaitsev said, "communicative civilizations with clear and non-paranoid planetary consciousness" why are we not hearing from them?

It didn't take the SETI folks to pose this question. Italian physicist Enrico Fermi did so two decades before that first meeting. His question became known as the Fermi Paradox. Summarizing that paradox recently, political thinker and essayist Charles Krauthammer wrote:

> *[The] silence is maddening—and not just because it compounds our feeling of cosmic isolation, but also because it makes no sense. As we inevitably find more and more exoplanets where intelligent life can exist, why have we found no evidence—no signals, no radio waves—that intelligent life does exist?*

Krauthammer suggests a provocative explanation for the Fermi Paradox. Might it be that intelligent civilizations inevitably advance toward self-annihilation? In other words, if one of the parameters in Drake's equation is the length of time an intelligent civilization exists, perhaps none has existed long enough to have overlapped with ours. Or as Krauthammer states in his essay "The Lesson of a Lonely Universe":

> *In other words, this silent universe is conveying not a flattering lesson about our uniqueness, but a tragic story about our destiny. It is telling us that intelligence may be the most cursed faculty in the entire universe—an endowment not just ultimately fatal but, on the scale of cosmic time, almost instantly so.*
>
> Philadelphia Inquirer, Jan 02, 2012

There is good reason to side with Krauthammer as his essay goes on to offer modern evidence that human beings and socio-political groups cannot peacefully satisfy their hunger for nor discipline their use of the technological powers that science creates.

In short, the trajectory of science and civilization is ultimately toward dystopia, not utopia—a self-destructive world, not a perfect one.

Even Sir Thomas Moore who coined the word *utopia* in his famous book of the same name (Utopia, 1516) unintentionally forecasted Fermi's paradox in a pun. He purposefully began his word with the letter "u" leaving off either of two letters that formed standard Greek prefixes. If he had spelled it *eu*topia he would have been using the word for "good place." ("eu is the prefix for "good" and "topos" is the Greek word for "place.") If he had spelled it *ou*topia he would have been using the word for "no place." By leaving the prefix letter "u" stripped of either letter, he builds the question into the very word *utopia*: *Is there such a place? Can there ever be such a place as a eutopia? Or is eutopia no place?* So he left both possibilities, the *e* and the *o*, out of the word.

Actually Moore thought it was possible and tried to describe how utopia might work. And modern human history is full of attempts at creating utopias. It is well known that the pilgrims came to America to find religious freedom. It is a lesser known fact that they attempted to create a utopia based on having no personal possessions and sharing all they produced. It was a horrible failure, one that the first governor William Bradford lamented for the laziness, injustice, and even starvation it created.

And these people were Christians!—people willing to die for the faith of their fathers, but apparently not willing to share the fruit of their labors. It was not until the community renounced the utopian plan and reverted to individual ownership that their fortunes were reversed and the community began to thrive.

Nevertheless, utopian enterprises persisted through the next two centuries in pockets here and there. And they still spring up today as well. Although, two world wars, nuclear armament, terrorism and widespread media exposure

> The trajectory of science and civilization is ultimately toward dystopia, not utopia—a self-destructive world, not a perfect one.

to incessant stories of human evil make it harder for any reasonable person to believe in the possibility of creating a utopia. We are more likely to trash the word and revive its Greek spelling *outopia*. And still...

Even in our modern era of cynicism, we seem to be unable to completely shed the utopian hope. Our movies and music from time to time still offer a description of what a utopia would be like. John Lennon's 1971 hit is a case in point:

> *Imagine there's no countries*
> *It isn't hard to do*
> *Nothing to kill or die for*
> *And no religion too*
> *Imagine all the people*
> *Living life in peace...*
>
> *You may say I'm a dreamer*
> *But I'm not the only one*
> *I hope someday you'll join us*
> *And the world will be as one*
>
> *Imagine no possessions*
> *I wonder if you can*
> *No need for greed or hunger*
> *A brotherhood of man*
> *Imagine all the people*
> *Sharing all the world...*

Could the fact that we can't shake the utopian dream indicate that human beings have a built-in belief in and a lingering longing for a *eutopia* somewhere that we were designed to help create?

The answer from scripture is a resounding yes. When God was creating the first *person* in His image, it was His purpose to also create a *people*—a whole world of people—who working and living together harmoniously would reflect the nature of God collectively. In this chapter I hope to help you see God's work of salvation through the lens of another paradigm that resonates with humankind's innate hope, the *utopian paradigm.*

If you remember, the perspective of *Just Ask: Volume Three* starts at the base of salvation's cross looking forward toward new, never-before possibilities God is creating, not backward to what He was correcting. As impossible as it may seem to our modern skepticism, God is creating utopia and He wants us intentionally involved. That utopia is described with an array of terms in the Bible, probably because no one metaphor, analogy or symbol can do the trick:

> *But you are a chosen people, a royal priesthood, a holy nation, a people belonging to God, that you may declare the praises of him who called you out of darkness into his wonderful light.*
>
> 1 Peter 2:9

Recognizing the array of descriptors that exists, nevertheless for the purposes of this chapter I want to group them all into one word—the primary biblical word—and let that serve as the container for our discussion of God's utopian plans. That word is *ecclesia,* the church. I invite you to begin to think of the church as God's plan for utopia.

To prove that point all we need to do is listen to some of the utopian ways in which the Bible talks about the church.

> *His intent was that now, through the church, the manifold wisdom of God should be made known to the rulers and authorities in the heavenly realms, according to his eternal purpose which he accomplished in Christ Jesus our Lord.*   Ephesians 3:10

Here Paul clearly declares what I am claiming. The church has been the final self-revelation goal in God's creation plan from before the beginning of time. Even though God displays His glory wonderfully through the splendor of heaven and earth, Scripture makes it clear He determined that the highest expression of His glory would come through the presence and inseparable unity of the church and Jesus Christ in the world.

*Now to him who is able to do immeasurably more than all we ask or imagine, according to his power that is at work within us, **to him be glory in the church and in Christ Jesus** throughout all generations, for ever and ever.* Ephesians 3:20-21

The eternal plan is for the church to be the utopia for which human beings were created. Of course, it has not yet achieved that status. But that's what God is in process of creating, with our cooperation.

In a real sense I hope this chapter leads you to be as intentional about pursuing (particularly in prayer, since that is what this book is about) this utopian goal, as Paul was about pursuing God's goal for him as an individual. Let's read his passionate personal statement but revise it with a collective perspective about God's ideal for the church (something Paul would certainly endorse.)

*Not that [we] have already obtained [this utopian ideal], or have already been made perfect, but [we] press on to take hold of that for which Christ Jesus took hold of [us.] Brothers [and sisters], [we] do not consider [ourselves] yet to have taken hold of it. But one thing [we] do: Forgetting what is behind and straining toward what is ahead, [we] press on toward the goal to win the prize for which God has called [us] heavenward in Christ Jesus.* Philippians 3:12-14

Before we move on to ask how we can cooperate with God's utopian plan, a brief description of this utopian vision for the church is in order. We can't spend long of course. This is not a book about the church, and a library of books has already been and will continue to be written on the subject of the church, called ecclesiology. But it's worth summarizing the utopian goal of the church by highlighting four primary ideals that we should be pursuing.

## REMARKABLE LOVE

Any self-respecting utopia has to be a world of love. Out of love flows everything else a utopia hopes to create: peace, justice, harmony, happiness, and more. The problem has always been that the sin nature of individual human beings cannot produce the kind of love that is necessary: love that is indefatigably self-sacrificing, love that does not break covenants, love that is not a respecter of persons (i.e. strangers and outsiders receive as much kindness and generosity as family members) and love that forgives the shortcomings and sins of others. The list can go on, but you get the idea. This is a kind of love whose headwaters do not flow from the human heart. It can only flow from a God whose very nature is love. But that is exactly what Jesus made possible on the cross. God's love from above can now flood our hearts, as we discovered in the previous chapter.

*Out of love flows everything else a utopia hopes to create: peace, justice, harmony, happiness, and more.*

This is what we must be pursuing if we are to cooperate with God's utopian plans. If we do, if we even begin to approximate this kind of love, the Bible tells us that the watching world will be amazed.

Is this really possible? Certainly—as long as we believe Jesus never commanded anyone to do something that was not possible. He is the one who called us to this utopian kind of love.

> *"A new command I give you: Love one another. As I have loved you, so you must love one another. By this all men will know that you are my disciples, if you love one another."* John 13:34-35

## RICH DIVERSITY

Perhaps nothing declares the glory of God with more splendor than the rich diversity of His creation. Why create 20,000 varieties of butterflies? Our creator seems to take pleasure in showing His wonders through the display of differences: "Look how I never run out of ways to make things unique!"

Not a single snow flake is ever the same. Nor is any fingerprint. Since the beginning of human history scholars estimate that there have been 110 billion people who have lived on earth. Not a single fingerprint was the same! Incredible!

That should tell us God is not going to want a church/utopia held together by uniformity, one that coheres due to the strength of commonalities. Rather, for the church to be a true utopia it will have to be a place of such diversity that it displays a miracle of cohesion that can be explained by only one bonding force:

> *[Jesus Christ] is the image of the invisible God, the firstborn over all creation. For by him all things were created: things in heaven and on earth, visible and invisible, whether thrones or powers or rulers or authorities; all things were created by him and for him. He is before all things, and **in him all things hold together.***
>
> Colossians 1:15-17

Unfortunately, churches tend to follow the easier path toward *homo*topia (to coin a word that may not be coin-worthy). *If only everyone was like us, what a wonderful place it would be!*

It's much safer and satisfying to be around people who are like us. So we cluster according to similarities (homogenous) rather than differences (heterogenous). But homogeneity displays nothing except the truth of the quaint expression "birds of a feather flock together." The world will never be amazed by that nor see any glimpse of the glory of God in such uniformity.

Yet that's what we unconsciously prefer, if not intentionally pursue. This must be resisted and reversed. Consider even the current younger generation that often prides itself in its embrace of diversity... Go to the churches they flock to. Try to find anyone over 30.

God is in the process of creating utopia. But He needs our cooperation since we are the ones to inhabit and sustain it.

## REVELATION ENVIRONMENT

The love and diversity of God's utopian ideal for the church leads to the fulfillment of His purpose for the church. We already noted how Paul expressed it: The church declares convincingly through its existence the "manifold wisdom" of God not only on earth but in the entire cosmos (Ephesians 3:10). The cosmic dimension of that mission is hard to wrap our minds around. So at least it's easier to determine how that revelation happens on earth: It happens through the church's environmental impact.

Scholars largely agree that the Wesleyan Revival in England in the 1700s was the longest running revival with great social impact. While no one would argue that it ever created a utopia, it did foster the end to slavery, produced hospitals, poverty relief services and widespread improvement in the moral character of England.

One major reason for its impact was the discipleship method of forming small groups whose goals were arguably utopian in nature. No one would claim that any of these groups ever became truly utopian. However, to the degree that the expectations and endeavors of the groups approximated some utopian ideals, especially regarding their spirit of inclusion and practical love for the poor, the environment created by those groups revealed the gospel of the Kingdom of God.

John Wesley himself was a product of the impact of a utopian-like environment. His journals reveal how he struggled with his faith and confidence in salvation in the early years of his ministry until he came face to face with the communal witness of the Moravians. His journal entry of January 25, 1736 gives just one example of their impact.

> *At seven I went to the Germans. I had long before observed the great seriousness of their behaviour. Of their humility they had given a continual proof, by performing those servile offices for the other passengers, which none of the English would undertake; for which they desired, and would receive no pay, saying, "it was good for their proud hearts," and "their loving Saviour had done more for them." And every day had given them occasion of showing a meekness which no injury could move. If they were pushed, struck, or thrown down, they rose again and went away; but no complaint was found in their mouth. There was now an opportunity of trying whether they were delivered from the Spirit of fear, as well as from that of pride, anger, and revenge. In the midst of the psalm wherewith their service began, the sea broke*

The church declares convincingly through its existence the "manifold wisdom" of God not only on earth but in the entire cosmos.

*over, split the mainsail in pieces, covered the ship, and poured in between the decks, as if the great deep had already swallowed us up. A terrible screaming began among the English. The Germans calmly sung on. I asked one of them afterwards, "Was you not afraid?" He answered, "I thank God, no." I asked, "But were not your women and children afraid?" He replied, mildly, "No; our women and children are not afraid to die."*

*From them I went to their crying, trembling neighbours, and pointed out to them the difference in the hour of trial, between him that feareth God, and him that feareth him not. At twelve the wind fell. This was the most glorious day which I have hitherto seen.*

Wesley made numerous other journal entries reflecting on his first-hand observations about the Moravians. Neither he nor they would have claimed the group had arrived at utopia, but their movement in that direction, intentional or not, reveals the nature of the utopia God is presently creating in the church. It's an environment that so clearly demonstrates a contrast with other social groups in the world that people are more easily persuaded God is real.

## RECONCILIATION IMPULSE

Ultimately, wherever human beings are involved, there will be differences that can lead to friction and fracture. That will be especially the case in a group that pursues the church's utopian goal of rich diversity. Consequently, there must be a unswerving commitment to prevent divisions before they occur or bridge them quickly when they do. That has to be more than an organizational mandate. A spirit of reconciliation must impel every person from the heart.

This, of course, makes great biblical sense. For the church itself is conceived in the unparalleled work of reconciliation through the cross of Jesus Christ.

*Remember that at that time you were separate from Christ, excluded from citizenship in Israel and foreigners to the covenants of the promise, without hope and without God in the world. But now in Christ Jesus you who once were far away have been brought near through the blood of Christ. For he himself is our peace, who has made the two one and has destroyed the barrier, the dividing wall of hostility... His purpose was to create in himself one new man out of the two, thus making peace, and in this one body to reconcile both of them to God through the cross, by which he put to death their hostility... Consequently, you are no longer foreigners and aliens, but fellow citizens with God's people and members of God's household... And in him you too are being built together to become a dwelling in which God lives by his Spirit.*

Ephesians 2:12-22

It's impossible to miss the grand utopian language in this passage all based on one category of divine work: reconciliation—bringing divided, even hostile, people together in unity, harmony and equity. This is how the utopian ideal of the church began. It is how it must be sustained.

To cooperate with God in this way requires a passion, an inner impulse to never let any difference or disagreement develop into division. Surrender personal rights, forgive quickly and completely, embrace differences gladly no matter what it takes or how much it costs in order to maintain unity:

*Be completely humble and gentle; be patient, bearing with one another in love. Make every effort to keep the unity of the Spirit through the bond of peace.* Ephesians 4:2-3

Now that we have taken a quick look at the nature of this utopia God is in process of creating, let's turn our attention to how we can cooperate with His utopian plans.

According to Jesus Himself, the church would be the locus of His on-going creative work after the cross. Remember the time Jesus quizzed the disciples about His identity? When they finally landed on the one true confession—You are the Christ—Jesus not only affirmed the confession but predicted His mission beyond His death and resurrection: "I will build My church" (Matthew 16:18).

How would He do that? If we can answer that question then we will find the perfect realm for discovering what we can do and particularly how we can pray with confidence, because we will have a clear picture of what He wants to accomplish. So here's my answer to how Jesus builds the church: *Look at how He made disciples.*

Most of the time when we examine Jesus' earthly ministry, particularly concerning His relationship with His followers, we say, *That is a pattern for making disciples.* Books galore have been written about Jesus' pattern of disciple-making so that pastors, churches and parachurch organizations can follow it. All of these books are insightful and helpful, but they are too narrow in their application.

What if—and I don't think there is any *if* about it—Jesus is not just showing us how He made disciples, but how He builds the church? I suggest we should say of His methodology not only "this is how you make disciples" but also "this is how you build the church."

Let's test this out by skipping across the surface of Mark's gospel to watch Jesus' disciple-making method and extrapolate some components of a church-building method as well.

## EDIFICATION BY REBUKE?

One of the most unnerving and perplexing things we notice when we examine how Jesus related to His disciples is the number of "learning moments" He created with mild and not-so-mild rebukes in the face of their failures, errant thoughts and bad attitudes.

No doubt Jesus loved His followers, and they certainly "felt" His love to some degree. But the fact remains we have very little record of Him giving words of encouragement. Whereas the words of rebuke are fairly frequent. Had Jesus never heard of the rule: *Give ten compliments for every one criticism?* Did He not realize what every dime store counselor advises: Cushion your criticism with words of affirmation first? "Peter, I know you're trying hard to do what's right and you usually do, but..."

The fact remains His rebukes were usually as blunt as a

> Had Jesus never heard of the rule: *Give ten compliments for every one criticism?*

Pharisee's forehead. If we're honest, most of us are kind of put off by that bluntness. We actually wish Jesus were as meek and mild as the Sunday School song said He was.

Rebuke is the grace that begins the process of repentance and renewal.

But that's our problem. Not His. We're the ones who don't appreciate the value and purpose of straightfoward rebukes. Probably the disciples, living in a different time and culture, weren't as rebuffed as we are in our hypersensitive culture that turns egos into egg shells.

Often the best way to improve is to reprove. That fact is actually built into the very gospel message which lays out the path to salvation and spiritual growth in two simple steps: repent and believe. And the order is vital. There is no believing without repenting. The heart/mind must turn away from wrong thoughts, attitudes and behaviors before it can even be enlightened much less transformed. Paul implies that necessary order when he writes:

> You were taught, with regard to your former way of life, to **put off your old self**, which is being corrupted by its deceitful desires; to be made new in the attitude of your minds; and to put on the new self, created to be like God in true righteousness and holiness.
>
> Ephesians 4:22-24

Putting off the "old self" is the necessary step before you can be "made new in the attitude of your minds" which is the necessary step before you can "put on the new self." But how does a person know when to put off the old self unless he or she sees where the old self is operating? That's what rebuke is for.

Rebuke is the grace that begins the process of repentance and renewal. Therefore, we can extrapolate that rebuke is also the beginning of edifiying (building up) not only individuals but the church. In short, "I will build my church" necessarily means "I will rebuke my people."

Having established the purpose for rebuke, we have now created a window into how Jesus builds His church and where we can focus our prayers to cooperate with Him. Just look at the times Jesus rebuked His disciples. He seemed to rebuke them in times they fell short in three key areas.

HUMILITY

One day the disciples were locked in a sharp dispute over rank and position that they wanted to keep secret from Jesus—probably because their guilty consciences already knew their attitudes were wrong. As Jesus worked miraculously among the multitudes, they probably enjoyed the benefits of feeding off His popularity. They could sense His kingdom coming, so they wanted to reserve their place right beside Him. But there were twelve of them and only two positions open: one on His right and the other on His left—the positions of honor. So they argued over which two of them outranked the others.

Even though they were trying to keep their voices down, somehow Jesus knew what they were arguing about so He had to rebuke them:

> *They came to Capernaum. When he was in the house, he asked them, "What were you arguing about on the road?" But they kept quiet because on the way they had argued about who was the greatest. Sitting down, Jesus called the Twelve and said, "If anyone wants to be first, he must be the very last, and the servant of all."*
>
> Mark 9:33-35

The native impulse of most human beings is to want to be at the front of the line, at the head of the class, or at least above average. Even people who are not pushing for position want their deference to be noticed and appreciated. Utopias will always collapse under even a feather's weight of pride. "Consider others better than yourselves" (Philippians 2:3) is the utopian motto. In order to build the church Jesus will always have to rebuke a lack of humility.

EMPATHY

As the disciples watched Jesus face the clamoring crowds and grew in their loyalty to Him, it is not surprising that they became protective. Perhaps their hearts were sincere, but their priorities were reversed. So Jesus occasionally had to rebuke them. Apparently in these cases the disciples weren't looking at other people trying to understand their situation and see them from God's point of view.

For example, they didn't understand how children needed to be near Jesus: *People were bringing little children to Jesus to have him touch them, but the disciples rebuked them.* **When Jesus saw this, he was indignant.** *He said to them, "Let the little children come to me, and do not hinder them, for the kingdom of God belongs to such as these. I tell you the truth, anyone who will not receive the kingdom of God like a little child will never enter it." And he took the children in his arms, put his hands on them and blessed them.*

Mark 10:13-16

On another occasion they were so concerned about making progress on their journey they prevented a blind man from having access to Jesus' healing power. And worse, one time their lack of empathy was made even more evident in their attitude toward Samaritans. Although they themselves were lower class people, they did not try to understand what it must have been like to grow up Samaritan—the butt of Jewish prejudice and bigotry—and why those Samaritans might have rebuffed Jesus. Instead the disciples wanted to repay their inhospitality by wielding what they thought was justifiable divine wrath.

*[Jesus] sent messengers on ahead, who went into a Samaritan village to get things ready for him; but the people there did not welcome him, because he was heading for Jerusalem. When the disciples James and John saw this, they asked,* **"Lord, do you want us to call fire down from heaven to destroy them?"** *But Jesus turned and rebuked them, and they went to another village.*

Luke 9:52-56

A successful utopia requires every person to see others through gracious eyes with a divine perspective—and here's the kicker—all the time! Usually a normal person has the ability to empathize with most other people to some degree. But once a person falls into a category that disqualifies him or her from common courtesy in the surrounding social context—women, the disabled, children, immigrants—the ability and desire to empathize fades.

Any lack of empathy draws a quick rebuke from Jesus. He wants the church to be utopian, so you've got to pay attention to any twinge of guilt about your attitude toward the needs, status or struggles of people you may be prone to neglect or disrespect for some reason.

## FAITH AS IMAGINATION

Faith is the ability to see something that exists in the realm of possibility before it does in the realm of reality. It is the capacity to think, *With God nothing is impossible,* and believe it. Faith, therefore, is a function of imagination. It gives substance to what the mind can conceive before anything becomes material. Faith is the currency of the kingdom. It purchases all "goods" and performs all "services." Without faith it is impossible to please God. So it stands to reason that Jesus woud be quick on several occasions to rebuke His disciples when they lacked it.

There was a time a distraught father brought his terribly tormented son to the disciples for healing. But they couldn't set him free from his demonically induced malady. This failure triggered one of Jesus' harshest rebukes:

> *"O unbelieving and perverse generation," Jesus replied, "how long shall I stay with you? How long shall I put up with you? Bring the boy here to me."* Matthew 17:17

People who cannot imagine anything beyond what they have already seen or experienced will never be part of a utopia.

The sharpness of His rebuke indicated the intensity of His expectation that the disciples should have been able to remedy the boy's problem. That prompted their desire to understand what they could have done differently. His response challenged them to increase their imagination of what is possible.

> *Then the disciples came to Jesus in private and asked, "Why couldn't we drive it out?"*
>
> *He replied, "Because you have so little faith. I tell you the truth, if you have faith as small as a mustard seed, you can say to this mountain, 'Move from here to there' and it will move. Nothing will be impossible for you.'"* Matthew 17:19-20

People who cannot imagine anything beyond what they have already seen or experienced will never be part of a utopia. They are the people who look at the way their church is, the way people act, the way things are going and grumble. They look at what has been and use that as the predictor of what will be. They create church budgets based on pledges rather than prayer. They look at teenagers and see trouble. Their motto is: *This will never change.* They may sing the Gloria Patri correctly in their communion services, but the version they really believe ends...

*As it was in the beginning*
*Is now and ever shall be*
*World without change*
*Amen. Amen.*

No utopia forms around people without imagination. You don't need to worry about it collapsing; it will never even get started.

So those three areas—humility, empathy and imagination—seem to be a focus of Jesus special concern such that rebukes were called for when His followers fell short. But let's go back to this matter of God's utopian plans and tighten up the connection between rebuke and our cooperation with the Lord.

## WE SHOULDN'T DO THE LORD'S WORK

One of the most common mistakes Christians make is to attempt to do the "Lord's work." I understand what we mean when we say that, but it is not our place. When Jesus said, "I will build my church" He meant just that: "I will" not "you will."

So what is our role? I believe it is incredibly helpful to understand that the way we partner with the Lord in doing His work is to play the role of John the Baptist. Like John we should ask the question: *What can we do to prepare the way of the Lord?* Clearly that was the Baptizer's chief concern. He saw his role in the prophetic words of Isaiah 40:3 and declared them to his followers.

*"I am the voice of one calling in the desert, 'Make straight the way*
*for the Lord.'"* John 1:23

There is also no doubt that his work of making the way straight was primarily a call to repentance. He and Jesus both referred to John's baptism as one of repentance. When people asked him what repentance entailed he gave some examples:

*"What should we do then?" the crowd asked.*

*John answered, "The man with two tunics should share with him who has none, and the one who has food should do the same."*

*Tax collectors also came to be baptized. "Teacher," they asked, "what should we do?"*

*"Don't collect any more than you are required to," he told them.*

*Then some soldiers asked him, "And what should we do?"*

*He replied, "Don't extort money and don't accuse people falsely —be content with your pay.*   Luke 3:10-14

To prepare the people for the redemptive ministry of Jesus he challenged them to turn away from life attitudes and habits that would be barriers to the Lord's work.

Using that principle, we should ask what we must do to smooth the way for the Lord of the church to create His utopia. If that were our focus, chances are much better we would be listening for His rebukes so that we could repent and remove all barriers to His entrance.

Utopia, as we have seen, is fundamentally a world of perfect love. It is a love that has no origin in the human heart. It is divine in both origin and nature. If it is God's will to create a utopian world of divine love coming down from Him and Him alone, then our sole focus must be to listen for His rebuke and turn away every time we fail in humility, empathy or imagination.

Can you imagine a world in which her people do not look to their own interests but to the interests of others (humility)? Can you imagine a world in which her people weap when others weap and leap when others leap with joy (empathy)? How about a world in which her people always see how to glorify God with praise in times of difficulty (imagination)?

These are among the core standards for utopia. There are others of course, but this gives you the idea of how to approach cooperating with the Lord. Since

Jesus is building His church, His Spirit will be quick to rebuke (usually quietly) so that, if you're listening and repent, you'll be making the way smooth for the Lord to create utopia.

## UTOPIA FOR THE SAKE OF THE WORLD

Make no mistake, the Lord isn't creating utopia just for the sake of the current citizens of the church, the people who are already insiders. His intention is that the whole earth will one day become utopia.

> *Then I saw a new heaven and a new earth, for the first heaven and the first earth had passed away, and there was no longer any sea. I saw the Holy City, the new Jerusalem, coming down out of heaven from God, prepared as a bride beautifully dressed for her husband. And I heard a loud voice from the throne saying, "Now the dwelling of God is with men, and he will live with them. They will be his people, and God himself will be with them and be their God. He will wipe every tear from their eyes. There will be no more death or mourning or crying or pain, for the old order of things has passed away."*
>
> *He who was seated on the throne said, "I am making everything new."* Revelation 21:1-5

Have you ever noticed that this new earth is *not* created "up out there somewhere" in a distant heaven? Rather it's created as the City of God comes down out of heaven to earth! Earth is destined to be the location of the ultimate utopia. But even though the fulfillment of John's prophetic vision is reserved for an unspecified End Time, it's method is not. This is how God does all His work, He sends heaven to the earth for new creation on earth. He sends His Son. He sends His Spirit. He returns to establish His throne. So why would we think He's not doing anything already to create the first stages of utopia now?

We won't get it perfect, but in the mean time if we adopt a biblically sound utopian hope, we will be prepared to make way for the Lord to produce communities of radically loving environments that do what Revelation goes on

*Imagine that! When we join together to form a church, we can be creating a utopian-quality environment that God uses to transform people.*

to predict: The world around us will be attracted to the light and glory of God on earth (Revelation 21:24).

That's what church is all about. It's about creating the foretaste of a utopian environment that has environmental impact on anyone who enters. That utopian environment in itself has transformative power. When people who are rude enter into an environment full of the fragrance of kindness and respect, they will wind up being changed. When people who are ungrateful enter into an environment where the atmosphere is full of praise, gratitude and words of affirmation they will wind up learning a new language of thankfulness.

When people who are disrespectful, or dishonest, or disoriented, enter into an environment where people are respectful and open and purposeful, their conscience can't help becoming hungry for those traits.

Imagine that! When we join together to form a church, we can be creating a utopian-quality environment that God uses to transform people. We aren't just coming for ourselves: to enjoy worship music, hear a sermon, learn a little bit, get some encouragement for the week ahead and try to draw closer to God. Church is not something we consume; it's something we create…together.

Church is a group of people who bind themselves together to create an environment in stark contrast to the world. An environment of light, not darkness. Of peace, not conflict. Of mercy, not condemnation. Of safety, not danger. Of equality, not bigotry. Of generosity, not greed. Of hope, not pessimism. Of health, not disease. Of joy, not sadness. Of service, not neglect. Of love, not scorn. Of grace, not shame.

This is what we are called to be part of. Can you imagine how many people in the world would love to be inside an environment like this? Any given church may not already be like this, but we each as individuals can imagine it and try to live that way long before our local churches come close. In other words we can act with a utopian impulse and vision.

Shortly after taking the pastorate I currently hold I met a struggling family with so many problems no one knew what to do for them or with them any longer. The church folks had tried. Sincerely. But the extreme awkwardness of the family due in part to the fact that two of them—the dad and the son—had Asperger's Syndrome kept them at a loss for solutions. The elementary school aged son's vocal outbursts during services were often disruptive. *Maybe they could sit up in the balcony and be less obvious?* That request, as gentle and well-intentioned as it was, nevertheless hurt their feelings and created a lingering resentment that I discovered when I met them.

That's when I learned more of their situation. They lived in near poverty, in a house that was falling apart around them, with cats overrunning the house and odor overwhelming any visitor. But I also saw their hearts for others and their hunger to be accepted. So I introduced them to my wife, and we began meeting together with them on almost a weekly basis for many months. Our goal was to see how we could help, but God's goal was to see if we could love and like them as He did. We know that was the case, because that's what happened.

As the months went on we showed interest in their interests. We helped them with basic life skills. We went to bat for them when the utility company turned off their electricity in the middle of winter. We taught them how to budget and stick to it. We understood when they messed up and began to help them learn how to pray. And trust the Lord.

But wow(!) their situation was the most complicated and hopeless I've ever seen. One challenge after another: medical problems, housing problems, job problems, financial problems, attitude problems. Look up the phrase "one step forward, two steps back" in the dictionary and you'd see their picture, I'm sure.

What could explain our sense of privilege in knowing them? The utopian love of the Lord who calls us toward love, humility, empathy and imagination.

Then one day after we had been praying together for the Lord to bring the onslaught of financial problems to an end as a gracious reward for their sincere efforts to handle their finances well—on a day when they were one step away from losing their home—they suddenly and quite unexpectedly found out they were the beneficiaries of an estate worth $325,000.

That day their lives changed. Not everything. Not the Asperger's. Not the many quirks that marked their personalities or relationships. But overnight their life went from helpless to hopeful, from extreme instability to financial stability that they still enjoy today.

They are not living in utopia. Nor are we. Our church is not utopia. I'm certainly not sharing this story as if my wife and I consistently, or even frequently, model utopian ideals. At least in this case we were moving in the right direction. But I tell this story, because that's how utopias happen.

If each of us, as many of us as possible, would embrace the people right in front of us with love, humility, empathy and imagination—don't avoid or gravitate to people we are naturally comfortable around—well then—let's see what the Lord will do.

That's how we cooperate with God's utopian plans.

Utopia. The world tries to create communities like this, and sometimes they pull it off for a while. But any utopia formed by human effort always collapses. Always. People without the Spirit of love coming down from heaven cannot sustain bonds of love and peace on earth.

This kind of environment takes the Holy Spirit. It takes a hungry people, desperate for our only hope for this beautiful environment. It takes people who are ready and listening for any rebuke when they fall short of God's glorious ideal, so that they make the path smooth for the Lord to do His incredible creative, utopian church-building work.

With this in mind, it's not hard to imagine how ready God is to answer every prayer you pray that cooperates with His utopian plans. Go ahead and turn to the application section. Use the sample prayers as your guide for practice and increased confidence in prayer.

The **utopian paradigm** focuses on the fact that God's purpose before creation was to create a world of people whose collective lives would glorify Him in the whole universe as one unified body that displays His wisdom and reflects His nature of perfect love.

## REFLECTION QUESTIONS

1. We all believe that individuals can "reflect" the nature of God. But why do you think it takes a utopian-quality church to do that best, such that the statement near the beginning of this chapter is true: "The church has been the final self-revelation goal in God's creation plan from the beginning"?

2. The idea of utopia sounds wonderful until you remember that it involves some of those people around you whose quirks, attitudes and actions often rub you the wrong way. Think of a couple of those people right now. (You don't need to share any names.) What would have to change in you in order to make a utopian church happen if they are in the picture?

3. What difference might it make in your life and church if you focus on doing John the Baptist's work? Where might you need to do that?

4. Of the three examples of rebuke in this chapter, which one might you likely hear from the Lord? One about humility, empathy, or imaginative faith?

## REPENT AND BELIEVE

Lord Jesus, I confess that when I think about the church it's usually about what *I* would like it to be or do better so that it is more pleasing and helpful to *me* and people like *me* that *I* care about. I hardly ever think about whether my church is moving toward a utopian environment that amazes the world by its remarkable love and rich diversity. Forgive me for not making it my top priority to help form such a community of believers. It really stretches my faith to think this is possible. But if this is the end goal of your creation plan, it must be something about which You will eagerly answer prayers for assistance. So help me. Help us. Amen.

Because the **utopian paradigm** reveals God's ultimate purpose to create a community of human beings whose love and diversity displays the "manifold wisdom of God" to the universe, you can pray any of the prayers below for yourself or others and expect a positive response from God. (Always remember to say please and thank you.)

**Prayers for a passion to pursue a utopian-quality church:**
- ✓ Make this my top-priority in how I make choices and conduct my life.
- ✓ Increase the number of people around me who share my concern to pursue utopia.

**Prayers for remarkable love:**
- ✓ Make me as generous and kind to outsiders as I am to my family.
- ✓ Let me not grow tired of placing the needs of others ahead of my own.

**Prayers for rich diversity:**
- ✓ Show me/us how we unintentionally exclude people who are different.
- ✓ Show me/us "where to start" to connect with people of other backgrounds, ethnicities or classes.

**Prayers for becoming a revelation environment:**
- ✓ Help my words and actions inspire others to join the utopian cause.
- ✓ Help me/us not judge others, but to invite them into an environment that can transform them.

**Prayers for a reconciliation impulse:**
- ✓ Help me/us be quick to spot and stop the growth of any seed of contention.
- ✓ Show me/us where we need to heal wrongs and divisions from the past.

**Prayers for the increase of humility:**
- ✓ Increase the spirit of deference—putting others ahead of myself.
- ✓ Decrease the power of preference—letting go of the way I want things to be.

**Prayer for the increase of empathy:**
- ✓ Keep me/us very sensitive to the struggles and disadvantages of others.
- ✓ Open my/our eyes to people on the fringes of our social groups.

**Prayers for imaginative faith:**
- ✓ Help me/us keep working toward utopia in faith even if we never see it our lifetime.

Now read the Sample Prayer that shows you how to take one of the above bullet points and expand it into a full prayer based on the utopian paradigm. It's a prayer that is guaranteed God will answer. After that, prayerfully think about where you might need God's help to pursue the love, diversity, humility and imaginative faith such a utopian-quality church requires.

## A SAMPLE PRAYER

Dear Jesus. Even after reading this chapter I still feel like it is a pipe dream, a pie-in-the-sky notion, and totally unrealistic. And yet, I get that we're supposed to be shooting for something that human beings can't create. And I get that "with man this is impossible, but with God all things are possible." So I'm asking You to help me take some baby steps in that direction. First I need you to do whatever is necessary so this utopia thing becomes my personal passion - that I will begin to care about that as much or more than anything else in my life. After all, if this is the ultimate thing you had in mind in creation and salvation, then it needs to be the ultimate concern in my life. So help me, please. Amen.

## JUST ASK ... WRITE YOUR OWN PRAYER

_____

_____

_____

_____

_____

_____

# CHAPTER SEVEN

# New Earth

"A society grows great when old men plant trees
whose shade they know they shall never sit in."
(Greek Proverb)

He never saw the fruit of his labor. He never even got paid for his years of work. But today the citizens of the United States enjoy the realization of his vision as they walk from the Lincoln Memorial along the spacious two-mile tree lined National Mall in Washington D.C.

Pierre L'Enfant had a vision to fulfill President George Washington's request to design a capital city for our fledgling nation in the 100 square mile rural area at the confluence of the Potomac and Anacostia Rivers.

L'Enfant, a Frenchman, came to the United States to fight in the Revolutionary War and eventually became a respected architect and civil engineer. He had a vision to create a capital city that would reflect the

L'Enfant never saw anything that resembled the fulfillment of his vision for Washington D.C. But as sad as that seems, you must keep in mind that he never expected too!

values and character of the new American republic. So he positioned the Capitol, the seat of the legislative branch of the government, on the highest point of land, a position reserved for monarchs in a European setting. But in this new democracy the people were sovereign, not the king.

He envisioned a wide-open space that invited the citizens to come to the seat of national power, also a gesture not familiar in Europe. This was a nation "of the people" where every citizen was equal, and the design of her capital city should declare that, L'Enfant believed.

He envisioned that spacious mall area being lined with monuments and buildings dedicated to the history and governance of the nation. However, rather than seeing his plans take shape he was maligned. Most people, except Washington, thought he was crazy. They wanted him to lower his standards and compromise his plans that they attacked as too expensive. They wanted him to raise funds through the sale of city lots. But he dragged his feet, knowing that land speculators would snatch up properties and spoil the overall design.

Eventually he lost his position, never got paid, and the development of the national mall area languished—for more than 100 years! Finally in 1901 Congress formed the McMillan Commission to oversee the massive conversion of the cow-populated mall area into the magnificent showcase of national history and center of federal government that it is today. Since that time L'Enfant's vision and plan has guided the work.

"We take it into account for virtually everything we do," said John Cogbill, chairman of the National Capital Planning Commission in 2008. "I think [L'Enfant] would be pleasantly surprised if he could see the city today. I don't think any city in the world can say that the plan has been followed so carefully as it has been in Washington."

Nice to know. Now. But poor L'Enfant. It's been more than 190 years since he died. He never saw anything that resembled the fulfillment of his vision for Washington D.C. But as sad as that seems, you must keep in mind that he never expected to!

Even if he had not been maligned and his plans proceeded unobstructed, he certainly knew in advance that the development of a project of that magnitude, the realization of a vision that elaborate and a dream that lofty could never have been completed before he died, even if he had lived to 100.

That's the most amazing thing! And admirable beyond words. There are people in this world who are willing to give themselves to efforts from which they will reap no benefit. What could a nation become if most of her people were like that? As the Greek proverb says:

*"A society grows great when old men plant trees*
*whose shade they know they shall never sit in."*

The Bible talks in glowing terms about such people as that. They are considered heroes of the faith.

*All these people* [Noah, Abraham, Isaac, Jacob, et al] *were still living by faith when they died. They did not receive the things promised; they only saw them and welcomed them from a distance. …they were longing for a better country—a heavenly one. Therefore God is not ashamed to be called their God, for he has prepared a city for them.* Hebrews 11:13, 16

Interestingly, the author of Hebrews even describes what they were waiting for. And it calls to mind something similar to L'Enfant:

*For [Abraham] was looking forward to the city with foundations, whose architect and builder is God.* Hebrews 11:10

Undoubtedly, the Spirit of God inspired this famous chapter in Hebrews, because the Lord wants these heroes of faith to mark out our faith journey. We also have the sobering privilege of working now but waiting for the fulfillment of a grand architectural design—a design not for Washington but the world.

In this final chapter of the third volume of the *Just Ask* series in which we are looking at salvation from the foot of the cross forward into the future to see what God wants to create, not just correct, it is fitting that we would close with a chapter focusing on a new heaven and new earth. As we have been saying all along in this series, understanding what God is wanting to accomplish through salvation is the basis for our confidence in prayer. When we know the heart of God, we know what to pray.

Clearly, history is moving toward a grand and glorious consummation. So let's see what we discover about our part in prayer as we look at salvation through what we can call the *new earth paradigm*.

## WHERE ARE WE HEADED?

The very first thing we must do as we look at salvation through this paradigm is to make sure we are looking in the right direction. The common perspective people take when thinking about heaven and earth is analogous to standing on terra firma and looking upward into the starry sky. Earth is down here. Heaven is up there. From a biblical point of view there is good reason to scrap that perspective. The new heaven and new earth will not be separated spatially. They are going to be merged into one...because that's what God initially intended, before sin severed the unity. The goal of salvation is to reunite the two as Maltie Babcock penned so clearly and accurately in his beloved hymn *This Is My Father's World*:

> *This is my Father's world. O let me ne'er forget*
> *That though the wrong seems oft so strong, God is the ruler yet.*
> *This is my Father's world: the battle is not done:*
> *Jesus Who died shall be satisfied,*
> ***And earth and Heav'n be one.***

So if you've got it in your mind that you're going to spend eternity "up" in heaven as opposed to here on earth, you've got another thing coming. Literally. The two shall be made one. Same place.

This may seem odd or even incorrect to you. Centuries of conventional thought about eternal life tells us that it takes place "in heaven." The only reason this strikes our minds as odd, or even incorrect, is because we are the product of a great divorce that has occurred throughout the course of Christian history.

Howard Snyder tracks the history of this divorce in his important work *Salvation Means Creation Healed: The Ecology of Sin and Grace—Overcoming the Divorce Between Earth and Heaven.*

In his book Snyder details the damage that has been done coming from several strands of philosophical thought (such as, Greek dualism) and cultural influences (such as, the merging of church and state under Constantine) that tended to divide the material and spiritual worlds. That divide went unchallenged and grew deeper and wider as history marched through wars and tragedies, thus reinforcing the view of the material world as evil and something to be discarded in favor of a "better place." This view has become so entrenched in popular theology that the hopes of most Christians are now based on sentamentalized and unbiblical views of heaven and eternity, which are often popularized in what we call (inaccurately) gospel music.

> *Some glad morning when this life is o'er, I'll fly away.*
> *To that home on God's celestial shore, I'll fly away.*
> *I'll fly away, oh glory, I'll fly away.*
> *When I die, hallelujah, by and by, I'll fly away.*

This may come as a suprise to you but the Bible does not talk about heaven being our final destination—ever. At least, not "heaven" as we think of it being "up there" separated from earth down here like the following old favorites do:

> *I've got a home in glory land that out-shines the sun.*
> *Way beyond the blue.*

or:

> *I'm satisfied with just a cottage below*
> *A little silver and a little gold*
> *But in that city where the ransomed will shine*
> *I want a gold one that's silver lined*
> *I've got a mansion just over the hilltop*
> *In that bright land where we'll never grow old*
> *And some day yonder we will never more wander*
> *But walk on streets that are purest gold.*

This common conception of our eternal life taking us away from earth and transporting us to a non-earth existence in a distant heavenly realm is unsupported by scripture. Instead, if anything, scripture forecasts an eternal merging where earth, albeit a new earth, is the final destination. Heaven comes down to earth.

> *Then I saw a new heaven and a new earth, for the first heaven and the first earth had passed away, and there was no longer any sea. I saw the Holy City, the new Jerusalem,* **coming down out of heaven from God,** *prepared as a bride beautifully dressed for her husband. And I heard a loud voice from the throne saying, "**Now the dwelling of God is with men, and he will live with them.** They will be his people, and God himself will be with them and be their God. He will wipe every tear from their eyes. There will be no more death or mourning or crying or pain, for the old order of things has passed away."*
>
> *He who was seated on the throne said, "I am making everything new."* Revelation 21:1-5

It is absolutely crucial to note that the above prophecy is found in the last two chapters of the Bible. It is the virtual final scene. All other scenes, no matter what the imagery, must be displaced by this one. Notice carefully that the new dwelling place—God's Holy City—comes *down from heaven* to the dwelling place of people. Notice also that the imagery depicts that city "dressed" as the bride for her husband (presumably the people on earth). According to Jewish custom the bride processes to her husband to live in a home the husband has prepared for her, not vice versa. So apparently this "bride-dressed" city is coming down to earth to stay. We'll talk about this more and its implications a little later. In short, the location of our eternal dwelling—the place where there's "no more crying there"— is the new earth. Again one of the old favorites got it backwards:

> *Soon and very soon,*
> *We are going to see the King,*
> *No more crying there,*
> *We are going to see the King,*

Actually, we are going nowhere. "The King" is coming here, to set up His throne here. To make a new earth here, because He's bringing heaven here.

But what about the few verses in the Bible that make it sound like we will "go" somewhere to be with the Lord, as in Jesus saying to the thief on the cross beside Him that he would be with Him in paradise that very day (Luke 23:43)? First, those texts refer to what happens after we die, but before the final resurrection of the body. Yes, there is arguably an interim "place" that our souls go to be with the Lord, a place He has prepared for us. But that is not our final resting place.

As to what happens in the End Times there is much speculation and little agreement about what some scripture texts mean. Take for example:

> For the Lord himself will **come down from heaven**, with a loud command, with the voice of the archangel and with the trumpet call of God, and the dead in Christ will rise first. After that, we who are still alive and are left will be caught up together with them in the clouds to meet the Lord in the air. And so we will be with the Lord forever.   1 Thessalonians 4:16-17

Some interpretations take the phrase "caught up with them in the clouds to meet the Lord in the air" as the beginning of our trajectory from earth to a heavenly location. Others say Paul was drawing upon the familiar custom of how subjects of a kingdom greet the arrival of their monarch: they go outside the city and escort Him enthusiastically *back into their hometown*. (Although, recently scholars have argued there is not enough imagery in this passage to conclude that this is the picture Paul is painting.) So the jury is still out on how to understand this particular text. When a scripture text is not clear by itself, it is best to revert back to the texts that have a primary position and clear meaning, as is the case with the Revelation 21 text we've already looked at.

The most important point is to recognize that the new heaven and new earth will both be new, at least in part, because heaven and earth will no longer be disconnected. Beginning with the substitutionary death of Jesus, the legal means by which heaven and earth can come together was accomplished. He, the Son of God and Son of Man, was in Himself the uniting of heaven and earth in one body. What was made possible spiritually will one day be made real physically in an actual new heaven and earth combined as one. But make no mistake, they will be forever united in the same "location." And the Lord will come here to make that happen.

## INDESCRIBABLE

The amazing thing is that the "here" will be a radically transformed material world somewhat similar to what we now experience but indescribably more glorious. In that regard the new heaven and earth united will be "similar but different" like Jesus' resurrected body was similar but different. He was the same (as in, somewhat recognizable) but remarkably different (as in, the ability to pass through walls). He still ate, talked, walked—normal things an embodied soul can do—but He could also float away in the clouds.

Consequently the Holy Spirit chose to use language of familiarities as the starting point for describing what the new earth will be like when it is transformed by merging with the city of God come down from heaven.

> *And he carried me away in the Spirit to a mountain great and high, and showed me the Holy City, Jerusalem, coming down out of heaven from God. It shone with the glory of God, and its brilliance was **like that of a very precious jewel, like a jasper, clear as crystal.** … The wall was made of jasper, and the city of pure gold, as pure as glass. The foundations of the city walls were decorated with every kind of precious stone. The first foundation was jasper, the second sapphire, the third chalcedony, the fourth emerald, the fifth sardonyx, the sixth carnelian, the seventh chrysolite, the eighth beryl, the ninth topaz, the tenth chrysoprase, the eleventh jacinth, and the twelfth amethyst. The twelve gates were twelve pearls, each gate made of a single pearl. The great street of the city was of pure gold, **like transparent glass.** …The city does not need the sun or the moon to shine on it, for the glory of God gives it light, and the Lamb is its lamp. The nations will walk by its light, and the kings*

*of the earth will bring their splendor into it.*

*Then the angel showed me the river of the water of life, **as clear as crystal,** flowing from the throne of God and of the Lamb down the middle of the great street of the city. On each side of the river stood the tree of life, bearing twelve crops of fruit, yielding its fruit every month. And the leaves of the tree are for the healing of the nations. No longer will there be any curse. The throne of God and of the Lamb will be in the city...There will be no more night. They will **not need the light of a lamp or the light of the sun,** for the Lord God will give them light. And they will reign for ever and ever.*

Revelation 21:10-11, 18-21, 23-24; 22:1-3,5

Passages like this invite a plethora of descriptions from writers and songwriters attempting to embellish the picture. But we dare not stray too far from what's stated here, not as a literal picture necessarily but for recognizing that the new heaven/earth will be glorious *beyond* what we know. Yet what we know is the starting point for imagining what it will be like. C.S.Lewis put it this way:

*The hills and valleys of Heaven will be to those you now experience not as a copy is to an original, nor as a substitute is to the genuine article, but as the flower to the root, or the diamond to the coal.*

The point is that God's plan for a new heaven and new earth, a plan conceived and initiated before creation, will take His people into an existence of which we have only the faintest hint. Everything has been moving in that direction, without interruption even by the intrusion of sin, and the Lord God will make sure it happens.

I can barely imagine how His heart must beat with anticipation. Even as I write this paragraph I have been away from my wife for two weeks—only two weeks. Yet, even during that short period of time, I have been planning for our reunion and am preparing a surprise for her when that day comes. It's a huge gift, but not just one she will enjoy. It's one I will enjoy, not only in the giving, but in what it means to *us*. It's a gift that represents something we love to do together. It's an extravagant gift of a top-of-the-line road bike. We love cycling together. Even in our 60s we have goals to accomplish together—riding a hundred miles non-stop for example. It's a gift by which I am trying to say, "You are my precious friend. I want us to be as one. Sharing everything." I can't wait for that day to come in just one week when I bring that gift into her world.

If that's the way it is for me, the Lord must be nearly bursting to bring heaven to earth, to reunite with us, and give us the extravagance of a dwelling place made of material that even allusion to the richest gems can't fully portray. So what do we do now if we know that day is coming? Do we just wait? Or...

## WHAT DO WE DO IN THE MEAN TIME?

At this moment I am keenly aware of my utter lack of ability to find words that capture the glory of the future that awaits us. But I have tried to say two things: this God-ordained future is one that remarries heaven and earth, and it is God's passionate plan to accomplish this by making earth our eternal, unimaginably glorious home. If this is the case, then I believe it is our privilege and responsibility to respond in two ways that inform our concerns, prayers and actions.

***Honor the Creator and His creation.*** I have traveled a lot during the course of my ministry life, speaking all around the country and in many parts of the world. Consequently I have been a guest in many different homes and cultures. I have learned how important it is, when coming as a guest, to honor my hosts by trying to do things the way they do. I eat the foods they place before me, even when I almost gag. I observe and follow their table manners and social etiquette. I make my bed and fold my bath towels the way I found them.

That's how you show proper respect and honor when you are a guest in a place that does not belong to you. It's a simple principle, isn't it? And it translates perfectly as a guide for how we should treat the natural world around us. We are not owners of the world. The Lord is.

*The earth is the Lord's, and everything in it,*
*the world, and all who live in it.*   Psalm 24:1

*The heavens are yours; the earth also is yours;*
*the world and all that is in it, you have founded them.*
*The north and the south, you have created them.*   Psalm 89:11-12

We are invited, welcomed and VIP guests on this earth. But not the owners! Therefore, we should observe the same protocols we do when living as guests anywhere: do things the way our hosts do. How does that apply to the Lord as our host? How does He do things? What does He care about most as it pertains to creation? Here's a quick answer: Among his top priorities are *form* and *function*.

We dishonor the Lord and His creation if we do not take care to observe and preserve the beauty—form and function—of everything He has created. This is not a book on ecology or the environment, so I do not intend to go into detail on this point. But the fact is that too many Christians, including myself, do not elevate environmental concerns to the same level as evangelistic and spiritual concerns. But we should. If we pay no attention to the forms and functions of creation—ecological conditions, ecosystem balances for example—and simply use and ultimately abuse the earth for our own wants and needs, we are no different than a bad house guest who disregards and disgraces the hospitality of the host.

I'm a road cyclist. To me there is nothing like a wonderfully crafted bike. The average rider is not aware of the complex science involved in the creation of a high quality bicycle. Geometry. Aerodynamics. Materials science. Chemistry. Mechanical engineering. It's not just a matter of slapping a frame, two wheels, a chain and pedals together. I have the privilege of owning a carbon racing bike. I recognize and honor that privilege by keeping the bike meticulously clean. I learn how to work on the bike so I can keep it tuned up on a weekly basis. I am careful to handle and transport it gently. I

We dishonor the Lord and His creation if we do not take care to observe and preserve the beauty—form and function—of everything He has created.

God has
salvation in
mind for the
earth as well
as earthlings.

make sure I operate it safely, according to best practices for such a lightweight carbon bike. In short, I want to keep it functioning at peak performance for as long as possible, because the bike and bike riding is that important to me.

But an $7000 bike is nothing compared to the incredible value, beauty, form and function of the natural world. The benefit to us in keeping our natural environment in top working condition far exceeds any benefit I will ever receive from bike riding. Yet I, and perhaps you too, do not have nearly the passion for preserving the indescribable wonder of the earth that I have for something like my bike.

As I said, the purpose of this book is not to talk about environmental issues or practical steps we can take to engage in so-called "creation care." This is a book on prayer, on increasing our confidence that God will answer our prayers. With this in mind, the prayers we need to begin with and trust the Lord to answer are prayers of repentance. Of course, prayers of repentance must be sincere. That calls for each of us doing more than pray; we must change our ways. In that regard, there are many good books in the Christian and secular market that offer good action steps. Explore those resources. Examine your habits and lifestyle.

However, the point is this: if you will truly repent—as in "changing your ways"—then the Lord will reward your sincerity with blessings that include benefit to the land itself. We have God's word on that from this famous promise:

> *If my people, who are called by my name, will humble themselves and pray and seek my face and turn from their wicked ways, then will I hear from heaven and will **forgive their sin** and will **heal their land.*** 2 Chronicles 7:14

The esssential interrelationship between the physical and spiritual realms couldn't be any clearer. Sin tears everything apart. God and persons. Persons and persons. Heaven and earth. People and earth. Earth and earth. For all its grandeur the earth itself is also sin-sick and needs to be healed. It's waiting for its redemption:

*For the creation was subjected to frustration, not by its own choice, but by the will of the one who subjected it, in hope that **the creation itself will be liberated from its bondage to decay** and brought into the glorious freedom of the children of God. We know that the whole creation has been groaning as in the pains of childbirth right up to the present time.* Romans 8:20-22

The earth is groaning as massive tectonic plates shift and volcanoes erupt. And howling, as animals tear at each other. And weeping, as festering microscopic parasites devour towering elms. But this physical torment will be brought to an end somehow in conjunction with the spiritual liberation of the children of God. God has salvation in mind for the earth as well as earthlings.

If we will humble ourselves, no longer exercising our God-given dominion like a slave owner, beating the earth into submission, extracting its riches, thoughtlessly spoiling its beauty—if we will humble ourselves and pray, then salvation comes to the land as well as to her inhabitants. This is the heart of God.

So there is already, even before the end times, a mysterious connection between the spiritual acts of human beings, like repentance, and the healing of the earth. That reality, then, provides the basis for a unique category of prayer activities in which some Christians already engage but which others find odd: cleansing and healing prayer for geographic locations.

At one time my wife and I lived where there was a street corner that had seen several violent crimes in a short span of time. Murder. Robbery. Blood was spilled there. So we joined with a small group of other Christians who chose to go to that location, stand and pray against the destruction that had taken place there. We prayed for the blood stain of those violent acts to be erased and for a thorough cleansing of the spiritual stain that may have been invisibly desecrating ground that belonged to God.

Admittedly, I felt a little odd doing it. I certainly did not want to turn into some kind of New Age, Mother Earth

There is already, even before the end times, a mysterious connection between the spiritual acts of human beings, like repentance, and the healing of the earth.

There are indeed invisible connections between the spiritual privileges of God's children and physical blessings for the natural world.

worshipper. But if there are indeed invisible connections between the spiritual privileges of God's children and physical blessings for the natural world, then I wanted to offer those blessings in faith.

You are free to make of that what you will. I'm really not trying to be weird. But at least we can agree on this: God loves everything He created. We should too by taking care of His creation respectfully, tenderly and gratefully. He desires to heal the earth along with earthlings.

One day He will finish His creation plan with the unfurling of an incredible new heaven and new earth. So why wouldn't He want us to engage in those healing and blessing prayers now with faith-filled eyes looking toward the ultimate cleansing and transformation of the earth.

Again I say, since it is God's plan to make this earth our eternal, unimaginably glorious home, we can and should begin now to honor the Creator and His creation. We can and should also do something else.

***Herald the King and advance His kingdom.*** There is a day coming when the Lord returns to earth to set up His kingdom here. God's "new earth" plan includes an incredible transformation of how the natural world functions. The new order of that coming kingdom may be incredible, but it is not inconceivable. A picture of this new "peaceable kingdom" is described by the Lord through the prophet Isaiah in the following famous text that talks about the end to all predatorial relationships:

> *The wolf will live with the lamb, the leopard will lie down with the goat, the calf and the lion and the yearling together; and a little child will lead them. The cow will feed with the bear, their young will lie down together, and the lion will eat straw like the ox. The infant will play near the hole of the cobra, and the young child put his hand into the viper's nest. They will neither harm nor destroy on all my holy mountain, for the earth will be full of the knowledge of the Lord as the waters cover the sea.* Isaiah 11:6-9

Natural predators will one day have no appetite for their natural prey. This is what Isaiah describes. If that is what things will be like "one day" in the future when the King and His Kingdom arrive in full force on the new earth, certainly He would be pleased to bless any effort we make to restrain and arrest predatorial practices on earth today. People toward people, people toward animals, people toward the land, sea or air.

Predation is about causing harm with no thought about the aftereffects. Thoughtless and purposeless destruction. Taking advantage for inappropriate and gratuitous gain. Where do we see that going on? That's where we focus our prayers for change and God's help.

When we side with the elimination of predation we are heralding the eventual arrival of the King of all creation and the kindgom He will establish on earth. We are in effect preparing the way. We are looking into the future and saying, "One day there will be an eternal kingdom that will function like this." And then we go about doing what we can to change our world and reveal glimpses of what our King will do.

In other words, our motivation to care for the natural world surpasses mere environmentalism. It is worship and witness. It is part of what makes possible the closing vision in the Isaiah passage, that *the earth will be full of the knowledge of the Lord as the waters cover the sea.* Apparently the absence of predation replaced by the peaceful coexistence of once natural enemies spreads the knowledge of the Lord.

So why not get started now? Why wait for some eschatalogical future? Helping the earth become healed and transformed reveals the glory of the Lord now and heralds the eventual coming of the Lord. In short, environmentalism done right can be evangelism.

Of course, whenever you start talking about environmentalism you find that everybody and his brother has different opinions about what needs to be the priority, what needs to be fixed and how to do it. Rather than trying to sort through opposing viewpoints, here's

> Certainly God would be pleased to bless any effort we make to restrain and arrest predatorial practices on earth today.

something only we Christians can do that doesn't require joining or scorning Green Peace: liberate the earth from Satanic tyranny.

I don't understand how it all works, but the Bible clearly portrays this world, including all creation and not just people, as being subject to the predatorial schemes of the demonic realm. It will remain that way until the dominion of the risen Christ is enforced by His church. Demonic powers not only destroy souls, they destroy soils. They will spoil natural resources, even water and vegetation, if that might pry people's grip from a belief in the existence and goodness of God.

Of course, most forms of natural disorder or disaster are not the work of demons, but some are. The demonic realm has the ability to manipulate the physical realm. That's why Jesus had to rebuke the winds and the waves (see Mark 4:39), which would be a strange way to relate to winds and waves if the storm had been only a natural phenomenon. But in view of the fact that Jesus was on His way across the lake and about to land on the shore of new territory unreached by the gospel with its soon-to-be-confronted battalion of demons, that storm must have been induced by enemy forces to keep Him away. The enemy of our souls can push Mother Nature to unleash furious forces if that will mean poking God in the eye.

That's where we come in. Through prayer and proclamation God's people invade territories in which the enemy is entrenched. He can be messing with people's minds or their crops. He may be in people's hearts or their houses. We can hasten the advance of God's kingdom by flushing him out of his natural habitat. That's what the Kingdom will bring about fully when Jesus returns, but that's what the Kingdom has started doing now. Jesus put it this way:

*But if I drive out demons by the Spirit of God, then the kingdom of God has come upon you.* Matthew 12:28

When my wife and I served for five years at a Christian boarding school, many of the students came from troubled backgrounds involving drugs and violence. After a couple years we discovered a pattern. There was always a flare up of strange occurrences and behavior about three to four weeks into a new semester after new students arrived. Some kids would have bizarre visions and terrifying night time encounters. Some experienced the sensation of being strangled in their beds.

Eventually we began resorting to a simple practice of going from building to building claiming possession of the premises for the Lord Jesus Christ. In some cases we gathered faculty, staff and students together at the entrance of certain buildings that seemed under assault to sing praise songs. One of our favorite "weapons" was Martin Luther's *Ein Feste Burg*:

> *A mighty fortress is our God,*
> *A bulwark never failing...*
> *And though this world, with devils filled,*
> *Should threaten to undo us,*
> *We will not fear, for God hath willed*
> *His truth to triumph through us:*
> *The Prince of Darkness grim,*
> *We tremble not for him;*
> *His rage we can endure,*
> *For lo, his doom is sure,*
> *One little word shall fell him.*

All we did was sing at the top of our lungs—we, the redeemed people of the King of all creation—and things changed. We saw no flight of mysterious dark shadows scattering from the building, but invariably students were no longer being traumatized at night and often there was a season of spiritual breakthrough in church services shortly after.

The enemy clings to buildings, not just people. The spiritual and physical world may be divorced in our theology but not in the world's ecology. Satan's cohorts can not only push people toward sinful passions but send thousands of pigs into a suicidal frenzy (Mark 5:13). We herald the coming King and advance His Kingdom any time we vanquish predators, even invisible ones!

When we look at salvation through the *new earth paradigm* and see that God's plan is to create a gloriously united heaven and earth as the seat of His universal throne, there is no doubt that He will say yes to any prayers we pray to:

- honor the elegant forms and functions of the natural order,
- to repent and heal wherever it is broken or being broken,
- to put an end to forms of predation, and
- to begin transforming it into an environment of peace and perfection that declares the knowledge of the Lord.

There is one caveat, however. Think back to L'Enfant who never saw the fulfillment of his vision for Washington D.C. When we pray and work for the end of predation and new expressions of a peaceable kingdom on this earth before the Lord returns, we should not expect tons of satisfying results. The work of prayer in this regard is like the labor of old men who plant trees under whose shade they will never sit. It is their love gift to the future. It is their act of faith. But working for an unseen future is the highest and most heroic type of faith.

This is a very lofty place for ending a three volume series on prayer. However, the very immensity of this final paradigm reinforces the point I made in the first volume. Our salvation is great, too great to be contained in the one paradigm that stole the show in Christendom a few hundred years ago—the judicial paradigm. While central to our faith, that view of salvation as *substitutionary debt payment* is only one way to understand what God had in mind when He sent His Son to die on the cross. So much more was going on than just paying the price for our sins so that we could live forever. Since that first book we have moved carefully through ten other paradigms that enrich our view of God's heart and increase our confidence in prayer.

So it couldn't be a more fitting end to my mission to broaden our view of the Lord's salvation than to pull the curtains all the way back for the most comprehensive view possible.

It is my desire that you will be there with me in this new heaven and new earth. And I pray that we will bring with us many people who discovered the Lord because we prayerfully pursued the privileges of salvation that come when we *just ask.*

The **new earth paradigm** focuses on the fact that God has ordained there to be a new heaven and new earth united in the future. The death and resurrection of Jesus Christ made possible the first stage of that incredible reunion and re-creation—a stage when God's people work together through prayer and the church to heal and protect the natural world, and work against all forms of predation to begin making peace and harmony happen on earth.

## REFLECTION QUESTIONS

1. What do you think about this idea that we are not bound for heaven "up there" but that we are bound for a new earth and heaven combined?
2. How would you describe yourself at this point in relation to the natural world? Are you a "tree-hugging" environmentalist? A sympathetic recycler? A nature gawker? An animal lover? An amateur botanist? Or if you were honest, would you say you have little heart connection with nature? Do you pause for sunsets or hardly notice unless someone points one out?
3. Try to identify at least one way in which you are not honoring "our Host" in the way you are treating the natural world.
4. Can you think of a location in your town or city where the land itself may have been spiritually contaminated by sin or destruction? Would you be willing to go there to pray for its cleansing and healing?

## REPENT AND BELIEVE

Lord Jesus, I confess that I have been lukewarm about caring for creation. I haven't seen the issue of environmental concern as something that falls in any category of Christian responsibility, prayer or worship. In fact, I really think of myself as an owner of the world around me, not its steward or protector. I am truly sorry. I see now that I have been like an inconsiderate guest in someone's home, tracking in with mud on my shoes. Forgive me. Amen.

Because the **new earth paradigm** reveals God's end goal of creating a new heaven and new earth reunited as the place for His eternal Kingdom and to display His unequaled glory, and because things are already moving in that direction, you can pray any of the prayers below for yourself or others and expect a positive response from God. (Always remember to say please and thank you.)

**Prayers of repentance for the neglect and mistreatment of the natural world:**
- ✓ Show me where I am wasteful and should begin to conserve natural resources.
- ✓ Give me a "garden" of some sort to tend—a place where I interact with nature and show my reverence for You and Your creation.
- ✓ Give me the courage to adjust my spending habits to avoid consuming products that are manufactured in ways that harm the environment.

**Prayers for new eyes to see the beauty and wonders of the natural world:**
- ✓ Slow me down enough so that I never go through a week or even a day without noticing the beauty and privilege of living in this world.
- ✓ Redirect my curiosity to learn and care more about the natural world than about movie stars, or famous athletes, or the stock market, or... etc.

**Prayers for awareness of places to concentrate my efforts:**
- ✓ Show me where I can go pray to reclaim desecrated territory for You.
- ✓ Give me discernment to see spiritual battles that might be disrupting natural systems and balances.

**Prayers against forms of predation:**
- ✓ Human trafficking and slavery; child labor
- ✓ Identity theft and fraud
- ✓ Deceptive marketing
- ✓ Animal cruelty: puppy mills, factory farming
- ✓ Destructive lumbering and mining techniques

**Prayers for perseverance and commitment to goals I will not live to realize:**
- ✓ Help me find and create reminders of the real world I am working for.
- ✓ Give me opportunities to speak up for this vision of a "new earth" I am beginning to work for now.

Now read the Sample Prayer that shows you how to take one of the above bullet points and expand it into a full prayer based on the **new earth paradigm**. It's a prayer that is guaranteed God will answer. After that, prayerfully think about where you might need God's help to keep working passionately and faithfully for the good of this earth and the new earth yet to come.

## A SAMPLE PRAYER

*Dear Jesus. I'll admit it. I am a consumer. All you have to do is look at my trash. I buy so many products. The packaging alone that gets thrown away fills two garbage cans every week! I know I contribute to the mountains of trash that continue to build around the world. But I don't know what to do about it. So much of what I consume and throw away is because it's convenient. I don't have time to be more conserving. When something breaks or gets a hole in it, I throw it away. I don't have time to repair things. I don't have time to make meals that aren't pre-cooked and packaged. Maybe that's the problem. Maybe there's a direct connection between being wasteful and being too busy. Well...there's no maybe about it. That's the heart of the problem. Please slow me down. Amen.*

## JUST ASK ... WRITE YOUR OWN PRAYER

_____

_____

_____

_____

# CLOSING THOUGHTS

With this *Just Ask: Volume Three* I complete a vision I had three years ago to help people become more confident in their prayers. I believe even more strongly than when I started that seeing the heart of God as revealed in His many salvation purposes releases in us a sense of permission to pray boldly, because we can know we're praying according to what He wants to accomplish. It's wonderful and amazing to experience the freedom that comes from this perspective!

I had an interesting experience in preparation for writing this last volume that is representative of everything I have written. I have mentioned in each of the Prefaces that I was able to work on this project over the course of three years. In order to complete each volume I needed to take one month of a three month sabbatical each year in January. In January 2014 I completed volume one. In January 2015 I completed volume two. And now I am just completing volume three in 2016.

As you would expect, going away for a whole month on my own requires much preparation and support from my family and church. Being a pastor of a good-size church means almost anything can happen that can force a change of plans. But this time, we had a different wrinkle—a wonderful one.

Our daughter and her husband were expecting their second child. The due date was January 7—one week into my scheduled and paid-for sabbatical. My wife and I contemplated the many adjustments we would have to make in order to be present if possible to help support them. I made the decision that I would leave my writing location and fly to be with them, knowing that I would give up four of the 24 days I needed to finish the book. Trying to complete it in 24 days is a tall order in the first place. The loss of any days at all jeopardized that prospect. But first things first...

Then my wonderful wife, whom I often call my prayer hero for the way she models faith and faithfulness in prayer started to pray a prayer that captures the word "just" in the title *Just Ask*. She prayed, "Lord, we are asking that Erin will deliver her child before the end of the year. Ideally it would be during the week right after Christmas and all our church and family festivities." When I heard her the first time, I interpreted it as her expression of a "wish." But then she kept praying it every night. Soon I jumped in with her to join her confidence in our Father's lovingkindness. It's not that we thought our prayers would force God to do what we were asking, but why not just ask?

We started praying this in early November, but I still bought refundable plane tickets to fly from Gulf Shores (AL) to northwestern Illinois on her due date. You see, we weren't trying to "claim" something. We were just asking for a favor based on the Lord's invitation and our confidence in His kindness.

Well, you guessed it. Sure enough Chase David Eckberg was born on December 28. It was perfect timing. I was able to be home to care for our elderly parents who live with us, so my wife could be there for the delivery. Then I was able to go up for when they came home from the hospital and head out the day after for my full sabbatical as scheduled.

That was a wonderful answer to prayer. Of course there is no way to prove a causal connection between our prayers and the baby's timely birth. We wouldn't make that claim. But here's the point: When answers to prayers like that happen on a frequent basis—and they do, for we also prayed our daughter would have an easy delivery in contrast to her previous 38 hours in labor, and she had an incredible 6 hour delivery!—there comes a point where reason says, "This happens too regularly regarding very specific prayers to be matters of happy coincidence."

So in closing I want to leave you with a prayer that comes out of the heart of this book, and encourage you to learn more and more about the kindness of the Lord and His great plans for you, so that you will not shy away from presenting your requests.

> *Lord Jesus, everything Your heart desires has been revealed in what Your Word tells us about salvation. So I will trust You and worship You by accepting Your invitation to present all my requests with prayer and thanksgiving. Counting on Your goodness as my heavenly Father, I will call upon you with simple but sound faith and just ask. Amen.*

CPSIA information can be obtained
at www.ICGtesting.com
Printed in the USA
FSOW03n0959190916
25168FS